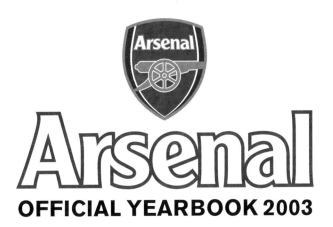

Arsenal

OFFICIAL YEARBOOK 2003

Acknowledgements

The editor would like to thank Julian Flanders, Joe Cohen, Andy Exley,
Stuart MacFarlane and David Price for their help throughout this project.

Produced for

Hamlyn by Designsection

First published in 2003 by

Hamlyn, a division of Octopus Publishing Group Ltd
2–4 Heron Quays, London E14 4JP

ISBN 0 600 60943 X

A CIP catalogue record for this book is available from the British Library

Printed and bound by

Butler & Tanner Ltd

10 9 8 7 6 5 4 3 2 1

Executive Editor

Trevor Davies

Project Editor

Adam Ward

Executive Art Editor

Peter Burt

Design

Lyn Davies and Rhiannon Sully at Designsection

Production

Ian Paton

All images

Copyright © Arsenal Football Club Plc / Stuart MacFarlane

Statistics

All statistics complete to 17 May 2003

www.arsenal.com

CONTENTS

key to match reports:

FA BARCLAYCARD PREMIERSHIP
UEFA CHAMPIONS LEAGUE
WORTHINGTON CUP
FA CUP
FA COMMUNITY SHIELD

DIRECTORS

Peter Hill-Wood (Chairman)
David Dein (Vice-Chairman)
Sir Roger Gibbs
Richard Carr
Daniel Fiszman
Ken Friar OBE

Managing Director
Keith Edelman

Manager
Arsène Wenger

Secretary
David Miles

MAJOR HONOURS

League Champions 1930-31, 1932-33, 1933-34, 1934-35, 1937-38, 1947-48, 1952-53, 1970-71, 1988-89, 1990-91, 1997-98, 2001-02

FA Cup Winners 1929-30, 1935-36, 1949-50, 1970-71, 1978-79, 1992-93, 1997-98, 2001-02, 2002-03

League Cup Winners 1986-87, 1992-93

European Fairs Cup Winners 1969-70

European Cup Winners Cup Winners 1993-94

FA Youth Cup Winners 1965-66, 1970-71, 1987-88, 1993-94, 1999-2000, 2000-01

CLUB INFORMATION

Address Arsenal Stadium, Avenell Road, Highbury, London N5 1BU

Club 020-7704-4000
Box Office 020-7704-4040
Recorded ticket information 020-7704-4242
Commercial Department 020-7704-4100.
Website www.arsenal.com
Information info@arsenal.co.uk

Junior Gunners 020-7704-4160/4150
Arsenal Travel Club 020-7704-4150/4160

ARSENAL IN THE COMMUNITY

t 020-7704-4140
f 020-7704-4141
e bnicholas@arsenal.co.uk

ARSENAL MERCHANDISE

The Gunners Shop 020-7704-4120
Arsenal World Of Sport 020-7272-1000
Mail Order Credit Line 020-7704-2020

Arsenal Museum contact Iain Cook on 020-7704-4100

MANAGER'S MESSAGE

There are many positives to be taken from the 2002-03 season. The overall consistency of the team continued to be remarkable. It was a record-breaking campaign; consecutive wins in the top flight of English football, Premiership records for unbeaten matches as well as all-time League record for unbeaten away matches and consecutive matches scored in. The attitude, concentration, determination and the commitment of the players were spot on.

During the season some of our performances were just fantastic. Many fans will reflect upon the stunning away performances at Leeds, Roma, Eindhoven, Birmingham and Manchester City as outstanding moments and to score 119 goals in one season emphasises the quality of our attacking play. I felt that we dominated the League for a large part of the season and we will learn from not winning the Premiership this time around. We will come back stronger.

The season ended on a high with more silverware. Winning the FA Cup for the ninth time in the Club's history and becoming the first team to retain the trophy for almost two decades is a truly great achievement. The team showed huge mental strength in overcoming Manchester United and Chelsea in the earlier rounds and responded well under enormous pressure at the Millennium Stadium against Southampton.

Finally, on behalf of the players and myself, thank you for your support throughout the 2002-03 season. You are like our 'twelfth man' on the pitch and that is never underestimated.

FA Community Shield
Sunday 11 August 2002 at the Millennium Stadium, 2 p.m.

ARSENAL 1

Gilberto 68

1 David SEAMAN
12 LAUREN
5 Martin KEOWN
23 Sol CAMPBELL
3 Ashley COLE
15 Ray PARLOUR
4 Patrick VIEIRA
17 EDU
11 Sylvain WILTORD
10 Dennis BERGKAMP
14 Thierry HENRY

Substitutes

13 Stuart TAYLOR
18 Pascal CYGAN
19 GILBERTO Silva (Edu) 46
20 Matthew UPSON
22 Oleg LUZHNY
28 Kolo TOURE (Bergkamp) 85
30 Jeremie ALIADIERE

MATCH REPORT

Another season, another trophy. The Gunners launched their 2002-03 campaign with a thoroughly merited victory over Liverpool in a feisty encounter which belied the renamed Community Shield's official status as a friendly. The prize was secured by a single goal from Brazilian World Cup-winner Gilberto Silva, a new signing who showed encouraging signs of integrating smoothly into the Arsenal set-up after joining the action in the second half.

Arsène Wenger's side began at an impressive tempo and Campbell might have earned an early lead but he nodded wide from a corner. Then Liverpool 'keeper Dudek produced three splendid saves in the space of a few seconds, denying Henry from 25 yards, then blocking Bergkamp's two follow-up attempts.

It was 28 minutes before the Merseysiders mustered a meaningful shot, and then Seaman repelled an acute-angled Heskey drive at the near post. Thereafter, Liverpool began to settle, but still it was Arsenal who pressed the more convincingly, and Parlour went close with a cross shot.

Soon after the break the Gunners fashioned their best chance to date when Bergkamp sent Henry through only for his low shot to rebound from Dudek's leg on to a post and away to safety. Thus reprieved, Liverpool enjoyed their most effective spell, but Owen miskicked when set up by Diouf, then failed to convert a Gerrard corner with the goal gaping.

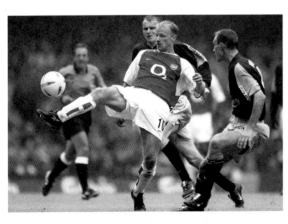

Dennis Bergkamp flicks the ball up and over Liverpool defender Sami Hyypia as Dietmar Hamann looks on.

0 LIVERPOOL

1 Jerzy DUDEK
3 Abel XAVIER
2 Stephane HENCHOZ
4 Sami HYYPIA
30 Djimi TRAORE
17 Steven GERRARD
16 Dietmar HAMANN
18 John Arne RIISE
9 El Hadji DIOUF
8 Emile HESKEY
10 Michael OWEN

Substitutes
22 Chris KIRKLAND
6 Markus BABBEL (Xavier) 78
23 Jamie CARRAGHER
13 Danny MURPHY (Hamann) 67
7 Vladimir SMICER (Owen) 85
28 Bruno CHEYROU (Traore) 88
5 Milan BAROS (Heskey) 74

Brazilian midfielder Gilberto marks his Gunners debut with the winning goal at the Millennium Stadium.

Arsenal reacted positively but when Vieira freed Bergkamp the Dutchman shot weakly and wide. Soon, though, he made amends by racing on to Cole's lovely pass, then pulling back to Gilberto, who swept home from 12 yards.

In reply, Liverpool mounted late pressure and Diouf's surge into the box was halted by a Vieira lunge. But the referee waved play on and Arsenal finished as they had begun – in control.

BOOKINGS

Arsenal Wiltord 23, Vieira 32, Henry 45, Gilberto 76
Liverpool Gerrard 6, Murphy 82

Arsenal make the perfect start to the 2002-03 season with a 1-0 victory over Liverpool in Cardiff.

FA Barclaycard Premiership
Sunday 18 August 2002 at Highbury, 4.05 p.m.

ARSENAL 2

Henry 9, Wiltord 23

1	David SEAMAN
12	LAUREN
5	Martin KEOWN
23	Sol CAMPBELL
3	Ashley COLE
15	Ray PARLOUR
4	Patrick VIEIRA
17	EDU
11	Sylvain WILTORD
10	Dennis BERGKAMP
14	Thierry HENRY

Substitutes

13	Stuart TAYLOR
22	Oleg LUZHNY
19	GILBERTO Silva (Bergkamp) 31
28	Kolo TOURE (Edu) 86
30	Jeremie ALIADIERE (Wiltord) 76

MATCH REPORT

Arsenal began the defence of their Premiership crown playing like Champions, turning in a fluent performance which was altogether too much for newly-promoted Birmingham City and which set a new record of 14 straight top-flight wins.

Frequently dazzling with the pace and polish of their movement and technique, the Gunners effectively destroyed the hard-working Blues in the first quarter of the contest, easing to a two-goal advantage which they never looked remotely likely to relinquish.

In all honesty, the opener was a gift, Johnson tripping Henry 32 yards from goal and the Frenchman's distinctly tame free-kick creeping under the groping Vaesen.

Soon the Belgian 'keeper offered some atonement by blocking Henry at his near post, but he was helpless to prevent the second strike, which was memorable even by Arsenal's modern standards.

Above *Ashley Cole jinks his way toward Birmingham's Jeff Kenna.*
Right *Sylvain Wiltord slides home Arsenal's second goal despite the attention of four Blues defenders.*

0 BIRMINGHAM CITY

18	Nico VAESEN
2	Jeff KENNA
26	Olivier TEBILY
12	Kenny CUNNINGHAM
5	Darren PURSE
3	Martin GRAINGER
22	Damien JOHNSON
6	Aliou CISSE
10	Bryan HUGHES
14	Stern JOHN
9	Geoff HORSFIELD

Substitutes

1	Ian BENNETT
17	Michael JOHNSON
24	Darren CARTER (Tebily) 60
11	Stan LAZARIDIS (Horsfield) 71
16	Tommy MOONEY

Cole, Vieira and Henry ferried the ball forward with delightful precision, Bergkamp's first-time pass found Wiltord on the left, and the livewire Parisian swerved inside past several challenges before netting with a sublime curler from the edge of the box.

That might have been the signal for the floodgates to open, but Vaesen foiled Henry and Parlour, then Campbell headed narrowly wide as the hosts assumed total control.

The early minutes of the second period brought little respite for Steve Bruce's men. Henry alone could have quadrupled his tally – one Vaesen save was of the highest quality – while Wiltord and Edu were profligate when presented with clear openings.

Around the hour-mark Birmingham rallied gallantly, but then Cisse was dismissed, for a second bookable offence, and the nearest they came to registering was a Carter header which skimmed Seaman's crossbar.

Instead of a credible fight-back, the closing stages brought a renewed siege on the visitors' goal as Keown went close with a header, then the heroic Purse, City's outstanding defender, made superb goal-line clearances from Parlour and Toure. In the end, the scoreline offered scant reflection of Arsenal's comprehensive command.

Thierry Henry displays typically mesmeric control to bring down an awkward pass.

BOOKINGS

Birmingham City Purse 23, Cisse 68

DISMISSALS

Birmingham City Cisse 74

WEST HAM UNITED 2

Cole 44, Kanoute 53

1	David JAMES
30	Sebastien SCHEMMEL
2	Tomas REPKA
7	Christian DAILLY
3	Nigel WINTERBURN
26	Joe COLE
25	Edouard CISSE
6	Michael CARRICK
8	Trevor SINCLAIR
9	Jermain DEFOE
14	Frederic KANOUTE

Substitutes

17	Raimond VAN DER GOUW
15	Gary BREEN (Winterburn) 69
19	Ian PEARCE
16	John MONCUR (Cole) 84
29	Titi CAMARA

MATCH REPORT

The Gunners battled back from two down in a compelling London derby. In the end, they went agonisingly close to the victory which would have set a new top-division record of 15 consecutive wins, though that would have been harsh on a West Ham side which commanded long stretches of the action.

Arsenal had started brightly and Henry might have registered with two early strikes, but he shot wide after a smart interchange with Bergkamp, then was foiled by James's dive.

However, the Hammers hit back potently and Seaman was deceived by a searing 22-yard volley from Sinclair, which crashed against a post and rebounded to safety, then the untended Kanoute shot high from 15 yards.

At the other end James scooped the ball from the toe of Wiltord, but the West Ham menace continued to grow and they took the lead when Kanoute combined neatly with Sinclair on the left before pulling back a low cross which Joe Cole curled home from 25 yards.

After the break the hosts became dominant and they doubled their advantage when Defoe centred for Kanoute's near-post stab to defeat Keown's lunge. The home centre-forward might have put

With the score at 2-1 to West Ham United, David Seaman pushes aside Freddie Kanoute's penalty to keep the Gunners in the game.

2 ARSENAL

Henry 65, Wiltord 88

1	David SEAMAN
12	LAUREN
5	Martin KEOWN
23	Sol CAMPBELL
3	Ashley COLE
15	Ray PARLOUR
4	Patrick VIEIRA
17	EDU
11	Sylvain WILTORD
10	Dennis BERGKAMP
14	Thierry HENRY

Substitutes

13	Stuart TAYLOR
22	Oleg LUZHNY
28	Kolo TOURE (Lauren) 78
21	Jermaine PENNANT (Parlour) 62
25	Nwankwo KANU (Bergkamp) 46

the result beyond reasonable doubt, but he was denied by Seaman and then shot wide – but now the Gunners stirred.

Vieira found Henry, who spun past Dailly and netted with an unstoppable 25-yard half-volley, an early contender for any goal-of-the-season award. Next Seaman saved Kanoute's weak spot-kick after Ashley Cole was adjudged to have fouled his namesake, Joe, thus setting the stage for the thrilling climax. Wiltord threaded a pass to Kanu, who shielded the ball for the charging Frenchman to sidefoot past James from 16 yards. Finally Toure might have snatched an unlikely triumph, only to be blocked by the plunging James, a suitably exciting end to a memorable match.

BOOKINGS

West Ham United Repka 63, Moncur 87

Arsenal Bergkamp 18, Edu 42, Cole 53, Keown 68, Vieira 75

Top, left *Thierry Henry evades the challenge of former Gunner Nigel Winterburn to crash home a 25-yard shot that makes the score 2-1.*
Left *Arsène Wenger was in animated mood at Upton Park, directing his team as they recovered to earn a point against the Hammers.*

FA Barclaycard Premiership
Tuesday 27 August 2002 at Highbury, 8 p.m.

ARSENAL 5

Cole 3, Lauren 21, Wiltord 24, 77, Aliadiere 90

1	David SEAMAN
12	LAUREN
5	Martin KEOWN
23	Sol CAMPBELL
3	Ashley COLE
19	GILBERTO Silva
4	Patrick VIEIRA
17	EDU
11	Sylvain WILTORD
25	Nwankwo KANU
14	Thierry HENRY

Substitutes

13	Stuart TAYLOR
22	Oleg LUZHNY
15	Ray PARLOUR (Kanu) 67
28	Kolo TOURE (Vieira) 79
30	Jeremie ALIADIERE (Wiltord) 82

MATCH REPORT

The Gunners were never in danger after blasting the Baggies with an early three-goal salvo, though the final scoreline did scant justice to a gutsy display by the Premiership newcomers.

The opening strike was devastating in the simplicity of its conception, exquisite in the precision of its execution. The instigator was Kanu, whose deft lob found Cole on the left flank; the England defender duped Moore, then bulged the far top corner of Hoult's net with a curling drive from the angle of the box.

Lauren was the next beneficiary of Kanu's creativity, the Cameroonian swivelling on to the Nigerian's neat delivery before crashing home from eight yards. Three minutes later the game ended as a meaningful contest when Wiltord raced on to Henry's subtle chip and dinked over the advancing Hoult for the third goal. The visitors refused to fold, however, and it took a desperate Campbell intervention to foil Roberts shortly before the interval.

Inevitably, perhaps, the Gunners' concentration appeared to dip in the second period, and Albion rallied valiantly. Balis and McInnes spurned scoring chances, then Arsenal's last man, Keown, was rather fortunate to escape with a yellow card after impeding Dobie. It was to the marksman's credit that he did not go to ground, and his subsequent

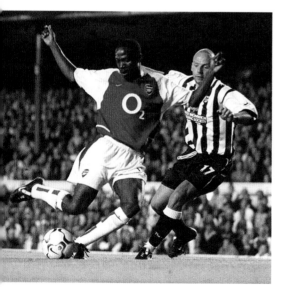

Lauren was one of four Arsenal scorers against West Bromwich Albion at Highbury.

2 WEST BROMWICH ALBION

Dobie 51, Roberts 87

1	Russell HOULT
2	Igor BALIS
3	Neil CLEMENT
6	Phil GILCHRIST
5	Darren MOORE
17	Larus SIGURDSSON
14	Sean GREGAN
10	Andy JOHNSON
4	Derek McINNES
12	Scott DOBIE
11	Jason ROBERTS

Substitutes	
21	Brian JENSEN
7	Ronnie WALLWORK
16	Lee MARSHALL (McInnes) 62
9	Danny DICHIO
15	Bob TAYLOR

Jeremie Aliadiere celebrates his late goal with Thierry Henry, who set up the chance.

shot was saved by Seaman.

The hosts restored their three-goal margin when Cole hared down the left and crossed for Wiltord to evade a challenge, then clip unerringly beyond Hoult from six yards.

But the Baggies remained defiant, and the pacy Roberts got the better of Keown before firing past Seaman from an acute angle. Arsenal's command was never in serious doubt, though, and Henry's threaded centre enabled Aliadiere to open his senior account for the club with a three-yard tap-in.

FA Barclaycard Premiership	27 August 2002	P	W	D	L	F	A	Pts
ARSENAL		3	2	1	0	9	4	7
Tottenham Hotspur		3	2	1	0	4	2	7
Leeds United		2	2	0	0	6	1	6
Liverpool		2	2	0	0	4	0	6
Fulham		2	1	1	0	6	3	4
Chelsea		2	1	1	0	5	4	4
Everton		2	1	1	0	3	2	4
Manchester United		2	1	1	0	3	2	4
Blackburn Rovers		2	1	1	0	1	0	4
Newcastle United		2	1	0	1	4	1	3
Charlton Athletic		3	1	0	2	4	5	3
Manchester City		2	1	0	1	1	3	3
Middlesbrough		2	0	2	0	2	2	2
Sunderland		2	0	1	1	0	1	1
Southampton		2	0	1	1	0	3	1
West Ham United		2	0	1	1	2	6	1
Aston Villa		2	0	0	2	0	2	0
Birmingham City		2	0	0	2	0	3	0
Bolton Wanderers		2	0	0	2	2	6	0
West Bromwich Albion		3	0	0	3	3	9	0

15

FA Barclaycard Premiership
Sunday 1 September 2002 at Stamford Bridge, 4.05 p.m.

CHELSEA 1

Zola 34

23	Carlo CUDICINI
2	Albert FERRER
13	William GALLAS
6	Marcel DESAILLY
14	Graeme LE SAUX
30	Jesper GRONKJAER
8	Frank LAMPARD
21	Enrique DE LUCAS
11	Boudewijn ZENDEN
25	Gianfranco ZOLA
22	Eidur GUDJOHNSEN

Substitutes

1	Ed DE GOEY
15	Mario MELCHIOT (Le Saux) 65
20	Jody MORRIS
12	Mario STANIC (Zenden) 71
9	Jimmy Floyd HASSELBAINK (Zola) 67

MATCH REPORT

After conceding a freak goal, then losing skipper Patrick Vieira to a controversial dismissal, Arsenal maintained their tradition of thriving in the face of adversity by fighting back to grab a point – and it was the least they deserved.

Deprived of Henry and Bergkamp by injury, the Gunners began steadily and were the more convincing team in the opening half-hour. Parlour drove wide after being set up by Lauren, then Cudicini parried a fizzing shot from Wiltord, which rebounded to safety.

At the other end Zenden might have done better than pull his shot wide from 12 yards after a right-wing cross from the enterprising Gronkjaer, but for the most part Chelsea looked lethargic until they went ahead in bizarre fashion. As Zola curled in a 43-yard free-kick from the left, Gudjohnsen's run distracted Vieira and Gilberto, who did not head clear; Seaman reacted too late, nobody got a touch and the ball bounced into the corner of the net.

Thus encouraged, Claudio Ranieri's men dictated proceedings for the remainder of the first period, and Lampard, Gronkjaer and Gudjohnsen all missed chances to increase their lead.

When Vieira was red-carded for a second bookable offence shortly after the interval, lesser teams might have folded. But, reacting positively to the apparent injustice suffered by the

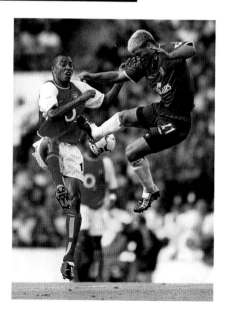

Gilberto braces himself for a painful-looking collision with Chelsea's Enrique De Lucas.

1 ARSENAL

Toure 59

1	David SEAMAN
12	LAUREN
5	Martin KEOWN
23	Sol CAMPBELL
3	Ashley COLE
15	Ray PARLOUR
4	Patrick VIEIRA
19	GILBERTO Silva
17	EDU
25	Nwankwo KANU
11	Sylvain WILTORD

Substitutes

13	Stuart TAYLOR
18	Pascal CYGAN (Kanu) 83
28	Kolo TOURE (Edu) 31
9	Francis JEFFERS
30	Jeremie ALIADIERE (Wiltord) 90

Frenchman, the ten men of Arsenal gradually assumed control and equalised through Toure. After wrong-footing two opponents on the left, the pacy Ivory Coast international slipped a pass to Cole, who crossed from the left; Wiltord's volley was repelled by Cudicini but the instigator of the move was on hand to head home from close range.

Thereafter the Gunners created the clearer scoring opportunities and Toure might have snatched a spectacular winner, but his howitzer of a free-kick, hammered from some 40 yards, narrowly cleared the angle of Chelsea's goal.

BOOKINGS

Chelsea Lampard 7, Le Saux 12, De Lucas 42, Gronkjaer 54, Melchiot 82
Arsenal Vieira 33, Wiltord 54

DISMISSALS

Arsenal Vieira 49

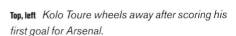

Top, left *Kolo Toure wheels away after scoring his first goal for Arsenal.*
Left *Ray Parlour chips forward under the watchful eye of Blues defender Graeme Le Saux.*

ARSENAL 2

Wiltord 26, Henry 42

1	David SEAMAN
22	Oleg LUZHNY
5	Martin KEOWN
23	Sol CAMPBELL
3	Ashley COLE
11	Sylvain WILTORD
19	GILBERTO Silva
4	Patrick VIEIRA
17	EDU
10	Dennis BERGKAMP
14	Thierry HENRY

Substitutes

13	Stuart TAYLOR
18	Pascal CYGAN
28	Kolo TOURE (Edu) 73
25	Nwankwo KANU
9	Francis JEFFERS

MATCH REPORT

The Gunners dislodged Tottenham Hotspur from the top of the table as the reigning Champions of the Premiership bested their First Division counterparts in an enthralling contest which was a magnificent advertisement for English football.

Playing with a spirit of adventure which is rare among visitors to Highbury, Manchester City contributed hugely to the entertainment, but though they stroked the ball around delightfully, Kevin Keegan's men were never as incisive as their hosts, for whom Bergkamp and Henry excelled.

The thrills began in the fifth minute when Seaman misjudged a Benarbia cross from the left, guiding the ball on to his crossbar instead of over it, but although City continued to press forward excitingly, they looked increasingly vulnerable at the back and might have gone behind had Wiltord not volleyed an Edu dispatch too close to Schmeichel.

Soon, however, the Frenchman took his revenge, racing on to a deflected Bergkamp through-pass before netting neatly from 14 yards. Almost immediately, the Blues hit back when a raking Benarbia cross from the right found Seaman in two minds, allowing former Gunner Anelka to equalise with a sharp downward header from six yards.

The Gunners reacted briskly and Wiltord was narrowly off target with a flashing header from Luzhny's centre and Schmeichel plunged nimbly to deny Henry. Meanwhile City continued to be enterprising, but were caught out when Wiltord freed Cole behind several defenders and the

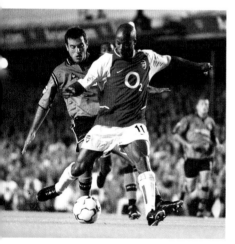

Sylvain Wiltord collects the ball in the Manchester City penalty area, takes aim and dispatches his shot beyond Peter Schmeichel.

18

1 MANCHESTER CITY

Anelka 28

1	Peter SCHMEICHEL
5	Sylvain DISTIN
24	Steve HOWEY
17	Sun JIHAI
29	Sean WRIGHT-PHILLIPS
3	Niclas JENSEN
23	Marc-Vivien FOE
8	Ali BENARBIA
14	Eyal BERKOVIC
7	Darren HUCKERBY
39	Nicolas ANELKA

Substitutes

20	Carlo NASH
22	Richard DUNNE
19	Danny TIATTO
6	Kevin HORLOCK (Howey) 78
10	Shaun GOATER (Huckerby) 59

England left-back's precise pass set up Henry to sidefoot home unerringly from 15 yards.

Further Arsenal pressure produced openings for Wiltord, Edu and Henry either side of the interval, but then Anelka tricked Cole and Edu before forcing Seaman to parry a scorching drive.

After 69 minutes a Bergkamp-inspired Henry strike was ruled out for offside, and City, though rather less dynamic in the second half, fashioned a late half-chance for Foe, who headed wide. In the end Arsenal were worthy winners though they never dominated, which was to the visitors' immense credit.

BOOKINGS

Arsenal Vieira 38
Manchester City Benarbia 22,
Distin 34

DISMISSALS

Manchester City Benarbia 85

Top, left *Thierry Henry hustles past City's Shaun Wright-Phillips.*
Left *Gunners full-back Oleg Luzhny drives the ball around Niclas Jensen and into the City penalty area.*

19

CHARLTON ATHLETIC 0

1 Dean KIELY
19 Luke YOUNG
5 Richard RUFUS
24 Jon FORTUNE
3 Chris POWELL
11 John ROBINSON
16 Chris BART-WILLIAMS
10 Claus JENSEN
21 Jonatan JOHANSSON
23 Kevin LISBIE
9 Jason EUELL

Substitutes

13 Paul RACHUBKA
6 Mark FISH
2 Radostin KISHISHEV
(Bart-Williams) 74
8 Jesper BLOMQVIST (Johansson) 67
20 Mathias SVENSSON (Euell) 74

MATCH REPORT

Imperious, irresistible Arsenal brushed aside a brave challenge from Charlton to retain their top spot in the Premiership, shattering a couple of long-standing records in the process.

The Gunners scored in their 45th successive top-flight match, thus eclipsing the mark set by Manchester City 65 years earlier, and they set a new club best of 27 League outings without defeat.

Through it all the skipper, Vieira, was at his best, controlling midfield. However, Charlton began spiritedly and might have broken through after four minutes but Johansson narrowly failed to reach a deflected shot by Bart-Williams. Arsenal, though, defused their hosts' early threat, then hit back when Vieira's cross was volleyed savagely by Wiltord from the corner of the six-yard box, only for Kiely to make a superb reflex save.

Shortly before the break Euell nodded wide from a Young dispatch, but a minute later the Gunners seized the upper hand when Vieira found Bergkamp on the right and the Dutchman pulled back to Henry, who netted with an unstoppable low drive from the edge of the box.

After the break the Champions assumed control, and almost doubled their advantage when Wiltord's clever dink was met by a firm sidefoot from Toure, only for the ball to cannon to safety off the foot of a post.

A second goal seemed inevitable, though, and duly it materialised when Wiltord rounded off a sweeping move involving Edu and Vieira

Left *Edu connects with Thierry Henry's cross to send a looping header beyond Charlton 'keeper Dean Kiely.*

3 ARSENAL

Henry 44, Wiltord 66, Edu 88

1	David SEAMAN
22	Oleg LUZHNY
5	Martin KEOWN
23	Sol CAMPBELL
3	Ashley COLE
28	Kolo TOURE
4	Patrick VIEIRA
19	GILBERTO Silva
11	Sylvain WILTORD
10	Dennis BERGKAMP
14	Thierry HENRY

Substitutes

24	Rami SHAABAN
18	Pascal CYGAN (Wiltord) 85
17	EDU (Toure) 63
25	Nwankwo KANU (Bergkamp) 71
9	Francis JEFFERS

from eight yards. It was the Frenchman's sixth goal of the season, which made him the Premiership's leading scorer.

Thereafter the Gunners could have added considerably to their tally but settled for one more, Edu meeting Henry's cross from the left with a precise looping header. Soon the Brazilian stabbed in again, but he was ruled offside.

BOOKINGS

Arsenal Keown 14, Cole 26, Luzhny 80

Above *Boys from Brazil... Edu celebrates his goal with compatriot Gilberto.*

Left *Arsenal skipper Patrick Vieira dashes across to close down the advancing Chris Bart-Williams.*

ARSENAL 2

Bergkamp 62, Ljungberg 77

1	David SEAMAN
22	Oleg LUZHNY
5	Martin KEOWN
23	Sol CAMPBELL
3	Ashley COLE
8	Fredrik LJUNGBERG
19	GILBERTO Silva
4	Patrick VIEIRA
11	Sylvain WILTORD
10	Dennis BERGKAMP
14	Thierry HENRY

Substitutes

13	Stuart TAYLOR
18	Pascal CYGAN (Ljungberg) 84
12	LAUREN (Luzhny) 73
21	Jermaine PENNANT
28	Kolo TOURE (Wiltord) 89
25	Nwankwo KANU
9	Francis JEFFERS

MATCH REPORT

Freddie Ljungberg resumed where he left off last season, returning from injury to seize a key role in the Gunners' successful opening to their Champions League campaign. The roaming midfielder was at his elusive best, helping to create the first goal and scoring the second himself, and the Germans never came to terms with his sudden untrackable runs.

Arsenal started at a fearsomely high tempo, with Henry's pace causing early uncertainties in the Borussia defence, but the visitors steadied and a Ewerthon shot was diverted disconcertingly close to Seaman's near post by Keown. In response Henry hit a firm cross-shot which Lehmann dived full-length to parry, then a superb four-man build-up climaxed in the Frenchman slicing wide from 16 yards. Next Ljungberg and Henry worked the ball neatly from the left, but Lehmann rushed from his line to foil Wiltord when a goal seemed certain.

All the while, though, Borussia were shading possession and twice before the break Fernandez threatened. The first time he was denied by a last-ditch Luzhny tackle, the second he fired narrowly high and wide from 25 yards.

Arsenal reacted positively and soon after the break Gilberto freed Henry, who netted only to be judged marginally offside. But the hosts' cease-

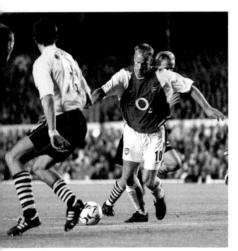

Dennis Bergkamp gets Arsenal's Champions League challenge off to a perfect start with a goal from 18 yards.

0 BORUSSIA DORTMUND

1	Jens LEHMANN
2	EVANILSON
21	Christoph METZELDER
23	Ahmed MADOUNI
17	Leonardo DEDE
5	Sebastian KEHL
6	Jorg HEINRICH
8	Torsten FRINGS
3	Juan Ramon FERNANDEZ
12	EWERTHON
9	Jan KOLLER

Substitutes

26	Roman WEIDENFELLER
15	Sunday OLISEH
7	Stefan REUTER
11	Heiko HERRLICH (Fernandez) 72
24	David ODONKOR
13	Guiseppe REINA (Ewerthon) 72
41	Leandro De Deus SANTOS

BOOKINGS

Borussia Dortmund Dede 14

lessly incisive movement paid off when Wiltord combined with Gilberto on the right, then passed inside; Ljungberg sold a delightful dummy and Bergkamp's 18-yard shot beat Lehmann via a deflection off Metzelder.

Now Arsene Wenger's men began to control the game and they doubled their lead through a counter-attack which was utterly perfect in its precision. Seaman threw out to Wiltord, who scampered down the right touchline and switched inside to Henry, who cushioned a pass into the path of the charging Ljungberg. The Swede skipped nimbly around Lehmann and stroked the ball into the gaping net, thus ensuring that three points were safely in the bag.

Fredrik Ljungberg salutes the Highbury crowd after his second-half goal.

Borussia 'keeper Jens Lehmann is left grounded as Ljungberg hurdles his challenge.

FA Barclaycard Premiership
Saturday 21 September 2002 at Highbury, 3 p.m.

ARSENAL 2

Henry 26, Kanu 90

1 David SEAMAN
12 LAUREN
5 Martin KEOWN
23 Sol CAMPBELL
3 Ashley COLE
8 Fredrik LJUNGBERG
15 Ray PARLOUR
19 GILBERTO Silva
11 Sylvain WILTORD
25 Nwankwo KANU
14 Thierry HENRY

Substitutes

24 Rami SHAABAN
22 Oleg LUZHNY
28 Kolo TOURE (Lauren) 84
10 Dennis BERGKAMP (Ljungberg) 68
9 Francis JEFFERS (Wiltord) 68

MATCH REPORT

Though considerably short of their free-flowing best, the Gunners dominated proceedings comprehensively, yet still needed an injury-time winner to claim the victory their superiority deserved. Such late drama might not have been necessary had Henry converted a 17th-minute penalty, awarded when Bergsson tugged Ljungberg's shirt. The Frenchman sent Jaaskelainen the wrong way with his spot-kick, only to see the ball rebound to safety from the inside of an upright.

Soon afterwards Henry might have made amends, but after outwitting Jaaskelainen and Bergsson in a chase for a long pass, he sidefooted wide of an empty net from a narrow angle.

Thierry Henry beats Jussi Jaaskelainen and fires into an empty net to open the scoring.

1 BOLTON WANDERERS

Farrelly 47

22	Jussi JAASKELAINEN
24	Anthony BARNESS
4	Gudni BERGSSON
16	Ivan CAMPO
25	Simon CHARLTON
3	Mike WHITLOW
13	Youri DJORKAEFF
14	Gareth FARRELLY
8	Per FRANDSEN
18	Dean HOLDSWORTH
9	Henrik PEDERSEN

Substitutes

30	Kevin POOLE
23	Danny LIVESEY
29	Stig TOFTING (Djorkaeff) 81
10	Jay-Jay OKOCHA (Holdsworth) 66
17	Michael RICKETTS (Pedersen) 48

Redemption was not long delayed, however, Ljungberg slipping the ball through to Arsenal's marksman-in-chief, who evaded Bergsson, rounded the Bolton 'keeper and this time he didn't miss with the goal gaping.

Parlour went close to doubling the advantage with a low shot, but shortly after the interval the Trotters levelled in freak circumstances. Charlton found Farrelly on the left and the Irishman dispatched a sudden steepling cross which sailed over the stranded Seaman and dropped into the net behind him.

Now the Gunners surged forward relentlessly, but for some three-quarters of an hour they battered Bolton incessantly without finding a way through. Henry curled just beyond the angle of post and bar following a Wiltord free-kick; Kanu went past Jaaskelainen only for his cross to be cleared; Henry netted from a Bergkamp pass but was ruled offside; Jaaskelainen held a glancing header from Kanu.

There were other near misses, too, but finally, deep into stoppage time and after Campo had been red-carded for a second bookable offence, the plucky visitors cracked. Cole delivered a deep cross from the left, Henry flicked on and Kanu poked the ball home from six yards. Highbury erupted in joy and relief.

BOOKINGS

Arsenal Keown 19
Bolton Wanderers Campo 8,
Holdsworth 55, Jaaskelainen 82

DISMISSALS

Bolton Wanderers Campo 80

Top, left *Kanu celebrates his late, winning goal.*
Left *Kolo Toure battles for possession with Bolton defender Simon Charlton.*

PSV EINDHOVEN 0

23 Ronald WATERREUS
30 Kasper BOGELUND
2 Andre OOIJER
3 Kevin HOFLAND
5 Jan HEINTZE
14 Johann VOGEL
6 Mark VAN BOMMEL
19 Dennis ROMMEDAHL
22 Wilfred BOUMA
10 Arnold BRUGGINK
9 Mateja KEZMAN

Substitutes

1 Jelle TEN ROUWELAAR
4 Ernest FABER
26 LEANDRO do Bomfim (Vogel) 27
16 Theo LUCIUS (Heintze) 61
13 Remco VAN DER SCHAAF
11 Arjen ROBBEN
8 Jan VENNEGOOR of HESSELINK
(Hofland) 46

MATCH REPORT

Arsenal put last season's European travel sickness behind them in spectacular fashion, crushing the Dutch League leaders mercilessly to record their biggest win in continental competition under Arsène Wenger. The victory consolidated their position at the top of their qualifying group, with maximum points from two games.

The Gunners got off to the perfect start with a goal after 21 seconds. Ljungberg found Henry on the left, the Frenchman skipped past Ooijer and squared for Gilberto to side-foot past the exposed Wattereus from six yards.

PSV reacted positively and almost levelled immediately when Bouma's cross was nodded down by Kezman, only for Bruggink to handle in the act of netting. Undismayed, the hosts continued to attack and Kezman headed over an empty net after a surging Rommedahl run, then shot past Seaman only to be judged offside. Cygan, who had joined the action after injury to Keown, was prominent in repelling several more Dutch raids, then Seaman made a brilliant save at the feet of Kezman, who was also narrowly off-target with a glancing header.

After the break, however, Arsenal took charge. Vieira and Henry combined to set up Wiltord but Waterreus blocked bravely, then Henry nearly registered with a near-post scorcher as the pressure built steadily. Eventually it paid off when Lauren chipped over the Eindhoven back-line and Ljungberg scored deftly from a tight angle with the outside of his right foot.

Dennis Bergkamp has eyes only for the ball as he races forward against PSV.

4 ARSENAL

Gilberto 1, Ljungberg 66, Henry 81, 90

1	David SEAMAN
12	LAUREN
5	Martin KEOWN
23	Sol CAMPBELL
3	Ashley COLE
8	Fredrik LJUNGBERG
19	GILBERTO Silva
4	Patrick VIEIRA
11	Sylvain WILTORD
10	Dennis BERGKAMP
14	Thierry HENRY

Gilberto and Bergkamp both spurned scoring opportunities before Henry buried PSV with a late double. First he exchanged passes with Kanu before darting between two defenders and sliding the ball unerringly past Waterreus, then a slick one-two interchange with Wiltord was climaxed by another clinical finish, thus capping one of the most authoritative and stylish displays in Arsenal's European history.

Substitutes

24	Rami SHAABAN
22	Oleg LUZHNY
18	Pascal CYGAN (Keown) 9
21	Jermaine PENNANT
28	Kolo TOURE (Ljungberg) 85
25	Nwankwo KANU (Bergkamp) 79
9	Francis JEFFERS

BOOKINGS

PSV Eindhoven Ooijer 20

Arsenal Lauren 34

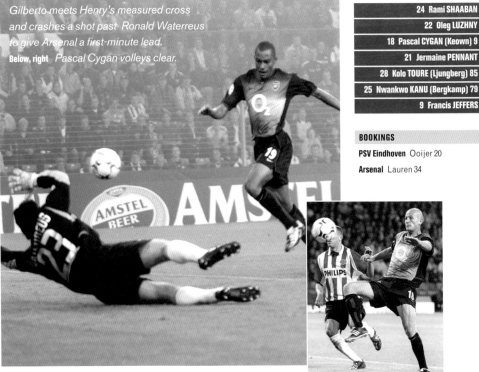

Gilberto meets Henry's measured cross and crashes a shot past Ronald Waterreus to give Arsenal a first-minute lead.
Below, right *Pascal Cygan volleys clear.*

LEEDS UNITED 1

Kewell 84

3	Paul ROBINSON
2	Gary KELLY
5	Lucas RADEBE
21	Dominic MATTEO
18	Danny MILLS
19	Eirik BAKKE
11	Lee BOWYER
4	Olivier DACOURT
10	Harry KEWELL
17	Alan SMITH
9	Mark VIDUKA

Substitutes

1	Nigel MARTYN
22	Michael DUBERRY (Radebe) 10
3	Ian HARTE
12	Nick BARMBY
14	Stephen McPHAIL (Dacourt) 46

MATCH REPORT

Awesome Arsenal outclassed one of their supposed Championship rivals, turning in the most commanding all-round display of Arsène Wenger's managerial reign to date. In defence his Gunners were diligent and solid, their midfield industry was matched only by its artistry, while the pace, precision and invention of the attack was irresistible.

The immediate upshot was a new record of scoring in 47 consecutive League games, thus overhauling the mark set by Chesterfield 72 years earlier, but the long-term consequences of such all-embracing excellence seemed even more significant.

Leeds were barely in the game after being breached twice in the opening 20 minutes. First Cole, robbed Kelly on the left, then produced a beautiful pass to Toure, who squared for Kanu to net from ten yards. Then Wiltord danced in from the right touchline, going past Mills and Dacourt before producing a perfect dispatch for Toure to double the lead with a firm eight-yard header.

Thereafter Arsenal were able to pace themselves, exercising constant control of the contest while occasionally raising the tempo and shredding their hosts seemingly at will.

Shortly before the interval Gilberto almost grabbed a third goal, but his flashing header from Henry's corner was cleared off the line by Kelly. However, the second period had barely begun when the margin was duly stretched, Campbell combining smoothly with Wiltord before Kanu

Kanu nips in front of Leeds' Dominic Matteo to score after just nine minutes.

4 ARSENAL

Kanu 9, 86, Toure 20, Henry 47

1	David SEAMAN
12	LAUREN
18	Pascal CYGAN
23	Sol CAMPBELL
3	Ashley COLE
11	Sylvain WILTORD
19	GILBERTO Silva
4	Patrick VIEIRA
28	Kolo TOURE
25	Nwankwo KANU
14	Thierry HENRY

Substitutes

24	Rami SHAABAN
22	Oleg LUZHNY (Toure) 72
8	Fredrik LJUNGBERG
21	Jermaine PENNANT (Wiltord) 79
9	Francis JEFFERS (Kanu) 88

played in Henry, who charged in from the left to slide the ball under the cruelly exposed Robinson.

At last Leeds rallied slightly and Smith met a free-kick from Bowyer, only for his header to smack against the Gunners' bar and rebound to safety. Eventually they registered when Kewell volleyed in from ten yards after Seaman had twice blocked drives from Bowyer, but Arsenal had the final word when Pennant's superb pass found Kanu and the Nigerian stroked home from 12 yards.

FA Barclaycard Premiership	28 September 2002						
	P	W	D	L	F	A	Pts
ARSENAL	8	6	2	0	21	8	20
Liverpool	8	5	3	0	18	8	18
Middlesbrough	8	4	2	2	11	5	14
Manchester United	8	4	2	2	9	6	14
Chelsea	8	3	4	1	15	11	13
Tottenham Hotspur	8	4	1	3	11	12	13
Leeds United	8	4	0	4	11	9	12
Fulham	7	3	2	2	12	8	11
Everton	8	3	2	3	11	11	11
Newcastle United	7	3	1	3	10	8	10
Blackburn Rovers	7	2	3	2	8	8	9
Aston Villa	8	3	0	5	6	9	9
West Bromwich Albion	7	3	0	4	6	11	9
Birmingham City	8	2	2	4	8	10	8
Manchester City	8	2	2	4	7	12	8
Sunderland	8	2	2	4	3	10	8
Bolton Wanderers	7	2	1	4	8	12	7
Southampton	8	1	4	3	4	8	7
Charlton Athletic	8	2	1	5	7	13	7
West Ham United	7	1	2	4	7	14	5

BOOKINGS

Leeds United Smith 6, Dacourt 17, Bakke 75, Bowyer 76

Arsenal Vieira 40, Campbell 48

Above, left *Pennant challenges England Under-21 team-mate Alan Smith in this midfield tussle.*

AJ AUXERRE 0

1	Fabien COOL
2	Johan RADET
4	Jean-Alain BOUMSONG
5	Philippe MEXES
3	Jean-Sebastien JAURES
8	Jann LACHUER
23	Olivier KAPO
7	Amdy FAYE
10	Teemu TAINIO
11	Khalilou FADIGA
21	BENJANI

Substitutes

16	Sebastien HAMEL
26	Jean-Noel DOUMBE
13	Stephane GRICHTING
6	Kuami AGBOH
27	Panxti SIRIEIX (Tainio) 90
20	Arnaud GONZALEZ (Lachuer) 73
14	David VANDENBOSSHE

MATCH REPORT

The all-conquering Gunners, so swashbuckling in recent outings, displayed a contrasting side to their collective character in claiming a second successive victory on the European trail. This time it was their superb organisation and discipline which caught the eye, though there was still enough flair on offer to construct a memorable goal.

Arsenal began briskly and twice in the first 12 minutes Cool charged from his line to deny the charging Henry. Toure, too, went close on two occasions during that opening salvo, first turning sweetly before chipping high from 25 yards, then shooting tamely after bursting through two tackles.

Next Kanu sent the whole Auxerre defence the wrong way with a mesmeric shimmy, only to shoot narrowly wide, but gradually the French league leaders gained a foothold. True, they lacked a sharp cutting edge, but before the break Benjani forced Seaman to make two smart interventions and Cygan was at full stretch to block the enterprising Zimbabwean.

The decisive moment arrived early in the second half when Toure skipped down the left and fed Wiltord, who swivelled past a challenge, then found the charging Gilberto, who shot firmly past Cool from eight yards. Auxerre attempted

Gilberto scores (left) *and celebrates* (opposite) *his 48th-minute goal.*

1 ARSENAL

Gilberto 48

1	David SEAMAN
12	LAUREN
18	Pascal CYGAN
23	Sol CAMPBELL
3	Ashley COLE
11	Sylvain WILTORD
19	GILBERTO Silva
4	Patrick VIEIRA
28	Kolo TOURE
25	Nwankwo KANU
14	Thierry HENRY

Substitutes

13	Stuart TAYLOR
22	Oleg LUZHNY (Wiltord) 83
26	Igors STEPANOVS
8	Fredrik LJUNGBERG
17	EDU (Toure) 60
21	Jermaine PENNANT (Henry) 58
9	Francis JEFFERS

BOOKINGS

AJ Auxerre Jaures 77

to hit back quickly, but Kapo nodded wide from a raking Radet cross and Cygan cleared a menacing free-kick from Fadiga.

At the other end Cool flew through the air to clutch a Wiltord header from a Kanu centre, before the dangerous Benjani twice threatened to salvage a point. First he wriggled past several challenges before unloosing a bouncing drive which demanded a sure-handed clutch from Seaman. Then, eight minutes from time, the England 'keeper tipped Benjani's sudden 20-yard scorcher against the crossbar, the impact of leather on wood resounding around the stadium before the ball cannoned to safety. After that, the Gunners survived further pressure with composure, thus moving to the brink of qualification for the second phase.

Left *Patrick Vieira strides forward purposefully as Auxerre's midfield retreats.*

FA Barclaycard Premiership
Sunday 6 October 2002 at Highbury, 2 p.m.

ARSENAL 3

Kanu 2, 9, Vieira 45

1	David SEAMAN
12	LAUREN
23	Sol CAMPBELL
18	Pascal CYGAN
3	Ashley COLE
11	Sylvain WILTORD
19	GILBERTO Silva
4	Patrick VIEIRA
8	Fredrik LJUNGBERG
25	Nwankwo KANU
14	Thierry HENRY

Substitutes

13	Stuart TAYLOR
22	Oleg LUZHNY
17	EDU (Wiltord) 77
28	Kolo TOURE (Ljungberg) 78
9	Francis JEFFERS (Henry) 77

MATCH REPORT

Two Kanu strikes inside the opening nine minutes reduced the Gunners' clash with troubled Sunderland into an overwhelmingly one-sided contest, and one which proved little more demanding for the Champions than a stroll in the Sunday afternoon sunshine. Along the way to a scoreline which did scant justice to their total superiority, Arsenal became the first club to go 30 Premiership matches unbeaten, annexing a record held previously by Manchester United.

The scoring began when Henry's near-post corner was scrambled away by Sorensen only for Kanu to drive it back and over the line.

Seven minutes later, the increasingly impressive Cygan found Ljungberg on the left, the Swede back-heeled into the path of Cole and the England defender launched a raking cross which Kanu headed home gleefully at the far post.

Soon Sunderland's gloom deepened as Sorensen was carried off with a dislocated elbow following an accidental collision with Henry and Craddock, and the Gunners continued their controlled domination of the game.

Wiltord saw two shots charged down, then another held deftly by Myhre, and it was the 42nd minute before the visitors launched their first effort on goal, Flo's shot

Kanu watches the ball bulge the Sunderland net after heading his second goal of the game nine minutes into the action.

1 SUNDERLAND

Craddock 83

1	Thomas SORENSEN
18	Darren WILLIAMS
17	Jody CRADDOCK
5	Phil BABB
11	Kevin KILBANE
21	Paul THIRLWELL
15	David BELLION
4	Claudio REYNA
8	Gavin McCANN
33	Julio ARCA
9	Tore Andre FLO

Substitutes

26	Thomas MYHRE (Sorensen) 17
27	George McCARTNEY
7	Matthew PIPER (Thirlwell) 59
31	Marcus STEWART
29	Niall QUINN (Flo) 75

Left *Kevin Kilbane attempts to halt Fredrik Ljungberg's forward run.*
Below *Patrick Vieira leaps over Darren Williams' challenge and accelerates down the left wing.*

from outside the area being blocked. Any vestige of doubt about the result was removed in stoppage time at the end of the first period when Henry touched a free-kick to Wiltord, whose scorching drive was parried by Myhre only for Vieira to nod in the rebound.

In fairness Sunderland, for whom the speedy Bellion looked intermittently enterprising, showed more signs of collective life after the interval, perhaps spurred on by a few well-chosen words from boss Peter Reid. But Arsenal seemed capable of cutting open their defence at will, and only a lack of urgency restricted the final tally. In the end, the Wearsiders did manage a fine goal, Craddock heading home from Kilbane's cross, but by then it didn't matter.

Kanu celebrates with team-mates Ashley Cole and Sylvain Wiltord.

FA Barclaycard Premiership
Saturday 19 October 2002 at Goodison Park, 3 p.m.

EVERTON   2

Radzinski 22, Rooney 90

1	Richard WRIGHT
28	Tony HIBBERT
5	David WEIR
20	Joseph YOBO
6	David UNSWORTH
26	Lee CARSLEY
16	Thomas GRAVESEN
12	Li TIE
11	Mark PEMBRIDGE
8	Tomasz RADZINSKI
9	Kevin CAMPBELL

Substitutes

35	Paul GERRARD
4	Alan STUBBS (Carsley) 90
22	Tobias LINDEROTH (Li) 55
18	Wayne ROONEY (Radzinski) 80

MATCH REPORT

Arsenal's marathon unbeaten run came to a stunningly abrupt and spectacular end at the hands of a 16-year-old prodigy. It was inside the last minute of a thrilling encounter in which the Gunners' craft had been just about matched by Everton's tireless graft, and with the scoreline appropriately level, that the astonishingly talented Wayne Rooney struck in dramatic fashion.

After controlling an awkwardly dropping pass from Gravesen, Rooney turned and struck a thunderous 30-yard curler which whipped past the blameless Seaman before nestling in the net via the underside of the crossbar. Then, as if to prove it was no fluke,

Rooney almost plundered another goal with an audacious chip which was only fractionally too high.

Such an outcome would have seemed inconceivable when Arsenal started in fluently dominant mode and took a deserved early lead. The architect was Henry, who shrugged off a posse of defenders before crossing from the left; both Kanu and Toure got touches as confusion reigned, and Ljungberg pounced to strike from eight yards.

At this point many teams might have crumbled, but Everton proved resilient, responding with a magnificent

1 ARSENAL

Ljungberg 8

1	David SEAMAN
12	LAUREN
23	Sol CAMPBELL
18	Pascal CYGAN
3	Ashley COLE
28	Kolo TOURE
19	GILBERTO Silva
4	Patrick VIEIRA
8	Fredrik LJUNGBERG
25	Nwankwo KANU
14	Thierry HENRY

Substitutes

24	Rami SHAABAN
22	Oleg LUZHNY
17	EDU (Ljungberg) 85
11	Sylvain WILTORD (Toure) 64
9	Francis JEFFERS (Kanu) 71

equaliser. After surging through centre-field, Gravesen switched the ball to Carsley, who struck Seaman's near post with a crashing drive from the right flank. The ball rebounded some 30 yards to Radzinski, who danced past Gilberto and evaded Cygan before netting powerfully from just inside the box.

The remainder of the first half produced thrills at both ends, with former Gunners custodian Wright repelling a bender from Henry and Seaman leaping to divert a Gravesen scorcher. After the break the impressive Dane brought another plunging save from the England 'keeper, but it was Arsenal who created the most openings. Kanu was blocked by Wright, Henry sidefooted tamely after fine work by Lauren, Wiltord shot against one upright and Ljungberg shaved the other. In the end, though, it was Rooney who had the final word.

BOOKINGS

Everton Weir 39, Pembridge 45, Linderoth 89
Arsenal Edu 90

Opposite *Thierry Henry resists the attention of Everton's Joseph Yobo.*
Left *Fredrik Ljungberg is brought to ground by former Gunners 'keeper Richard Wright.*

ARSENAL 1

Kanu 53

1 David SEAMAN
12 LAUREN
23 Sol CAMPBELL
18 Pascal CYGAN
3 Ashley COLE
11 Sylvain WILTORD
19 GILBERTO Silva
4 Patrick VIEIRA
8 Fredrik LJUNGBERG
25 Nwankwo KANU
14 Thierry HENRY

Substitutes

24 Rami SHAABAN
22 Oleg LUZHNY
26 Igors STEPANOVS
17 EDU
21 Jermaine PENNANT
7 Robert PIRES (Gilberto) 72
28 Kolo TOURE (Lauren) 77

MATCH REPORT

Though the slick surface at rain-lashed Highbury seemed ideal for the Gunners' flowing style, it was the French visitors who took early advantage, almost breaking through in the fifth minute when the ball ran loose after Seaman had plunged at the feet of Benjani and Lachuer volleyed wildly over a gaping net.

Three minutes later Auxerre took the lead in sensational style when Kapo nutmegged Vieira on the right before unloosing a low, high-velocity curler which Seaman touched but could not repel.

Arsenal responded in stirring style, Henry sprinting past several defenders, then pulling back to Kanu, who fired wide from 25 yards. Soon the Nigerian went even closer from a similar distance, shaving an upright after smart work by Vieira and Cole, but just as the counter-offensive was gaining momentum, the visitors struck again. Centre-back Boumsong rampaged forward, the ball broke

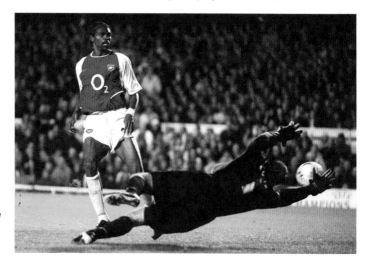

Kanu watches anxiously as Fabien Cool stretches forlornly in an effort to repel the Nigerian strikers's goal- bound shot.

2 AJ AUXERRE

Kapo 8, Fadiga 27

1	Fabien COOL
21	Johan RADET
4	Jean-Alain BOUMSONG
5	Philippe MEXES
3	Jean-Sebastien JAURES
8	Jann LACHUER
10	Teemu TAINIO
7	Amdy FAYE
9	Khalilou FADIGA
23	Olivier KAPO
21	BENJANI

Substitutes

16	Sebastien HAMEL
26	Jean-Noel DOUMBE
13	Stephane GRICHTING
18	Lionel MATHIS
27	Panxti SIRIEIX
20	Arnaud GONZALES
19	Nicolas MARIN

Robert Pires returns to first-team action after more than six months on the sidelines.

fortunately for Fadiga and the Senegalese dinked neatly over the stranded Seaman from ten yards.

The Gunners might have reduced the arrears when Gilberto and Wiltord combined sweetly to set up Kanu, but again the Nigerian shot narrowly the wrong side of a post. The second half brought more concerted pressure from the hosts and soon the deficit was halved when Lauren released Henry on the right and Kanu tapped in his precise cross.

BOOKINGS

Arsenal Campbell 68, Vieira 87

AJ Auxerre Boumsong 42, Faye 56

However, Auxerre almost restored the two-goal margin when a Cole miskick set off a pinball sequence in the Arsenal box which was ended by Seaman's splendid block from a Benjani drive.

Thereafter, though Arsène Wenger's men attacked relentless-ly, they lacked their usual penetration and the closest they came to equalising was when Pires, welcomed back after his lengthy injury absence, fired a fierce snap-shot straight at Cool during stoppage time. The return of the football writers' Player of the Year was the only positive to come out of an otherwise forgettable night at Highbury.

FA Barclaycard Premiership
Saturday 26 October 2002 at Highbury, 3 p.m.

ARSENAL 1

Edu 45

| 1 David SEAMAN |
| 12 LAUREN |
| 23 Sol CAMPBELL |
| 18 Pascal CYGAN |
| 3 Ashley COLE |
| 11 Sylvain WILTORD |
| 19 GILBERTO Silva |
| 17 EDU |
| 8 Fredrik LJUNGBERG |
| 25 Nwankwo KANU |
| 14 Thierry HENRY |

Substitutes

| 13 Stuart TAYLOR |
| 22 Oleg LUZHNY |
| 28 Kolo TOURE (Cole) 85 |
| 7 Robert PIRES (Edu) 64 |
| 10 Dennis BERGKAMP (Kanu) 64 |

MATCH REPORT

Despite the scoreline, the Gunners were in commanding form, creating no fewer than 27 openings and directing 14 of them on target, while Blackburn managed only four goal attempts.

Of course, the only statistic which mattered was that Graeme Souness's men converted 50 per cent of their chances, while only once could Henry, Wiltord and company get past the inspired Friedel, who performed a succession of near-miracles between the visitors' posts.

The Gunners began at a searing tempo with Wiltord's rasping drive demanding a smart save from Friedel, then the lively Frenchman shaved the crossbar with a spectacular volley. But soon they fell behind in freakish circumstances when Ostenstad escaped the attentions of Campbell and Cygan to feed Yorke, whose cross was miscued by Edu and the ball looped into the net beyond the helpless Seaman.

Ashley Cole chips forward as Blackburn's David Dunn attempts to block.

Without breaking their collective stride, Arsenal launched wave after wave of attack: Henry's cross-shot bobbled wide after Friedel had slipped, a prone Berg cleared off the line from Cole and the Rovers 'keeper saved with his legs from Wiltord.

Shortly before the break, the Gunners' luck changed when Edu's curling free-kick from the right eluded everyone and cannoned into goal off the far post, but Blackburn regained their lead early in the second period when Tugay's through-ball found Ostenstad, who switched it to the unmarked Yorke, and the Tobagan dinked neatly over Seaman.

2 BLACKBURN ROVERS

Edu og 6, Yorke 51

1	Brad FRIEDEL
2	Lucas NEILL
25	Henning BERG
21	Martin TAYLOR
14	Nils-Eric JOHANSSON
20	David THOMPSON
7	Garry FLITCROFT
3	Kerimoglu TUGAY
8	David DUNN
19	Dwight YORKE
22	Egil OSTENSTAD

That was the signal for Arsenal to mount a siege, but Friedel almost defied belief to repel a Campbell header, Pires fired high from 20 yards, then the 'keeper pawed away a Bergkamp screamer and a sweetly-struck free-kick from Henry. Finally Friedel parried a close-range drive from Wiltord, whose follow-up header was deflected against a post by Taylor. It just wasn't Arsenal's day.

Substitutes

13	Alan KELLY
6	Craig SHORT (Ostenstad) 83
18	Keith GILLESPIE (Tugay) 66
10	Matt JANSEN (Dunn) 85
12	Corrado GRABBI

BOOKINGS

Arsenal Henry 83
Blackburn Rovers Ostenstad 37, Johansson 45, Flitcroft 70

DISMISSALS

Blackburn Rovers Flitcroft 79

Left *Thierry Henry attempts an acrobatic volleyed cross.* **Far left** *Edu gives thanks after his goal cancelled out his earlier own-goal.*

BORUSSIA DORTMUND   2

Gilberto og 38, Rosicky pen 62

1	Jens LEHMANN
2	EVANILSON
3	Sebastian KEHL
21	Christoph METZELDER
4	Christian WORNS
17	Leonardo DEDE
8	Torsten FRINGS
18	Lars RICKEN
12	EWERTHON
10	Tomas ROSICKY
9	Jan KOLLER

Substitutes

28	Roman WEIDENFELLER
23	Ahmed MADOUNI (Rosicky) 90
6	Jorg HEINRICH (Ricken) 84
7	Stefan REUTER (Kehl) 69
22	Marcio AMOROSO
11	Heiko HERRLICH
41	Leandro SANTOS

MATCH REPORT

The Gunners' joy at reaching the last 16 of the Champions League was tempered by defeat at the Westfalenstadion. In truth, although Arsenal scored the first goal, the in-form Germans deserved their triumph, which moved them to the top of the qualifying group.

Borussia began at a high tempo and might have snatched the lead after only 70 seconds when a Ewerthon through-pass sent Ricken scampering between Campbell and Cygan. As he side-footed past Seaman a goal seemed inevitable, but the ball rebounded to safety off the foot of a post. After the England, 'keeper had fielded a low drive from Rosicky, the visitors were granted another narrow escape. This time Dede broke free on the left, his tantalising cross was nodded against the inside of an upright by Koller and again the ball was smuggled clear.

However, the under-fire Gunners broke the siege in the best possible fashion, Henry curling an exquisite 25-yard free-kick over the defensive wall and past the immobile Lehmann.

Though Borussia continued to dominate territorially, Arsenal went agonisingly close to doubling their advantage after 27 minutes when Ljungberg surged through the centre and the overlapping Vieira fired narrowly wide from 15 yards.

The hosts were not to be denied, though, and after Ewerthon had been fouled, Rosicky arced in a free-kick which grazed the head of Gilberto and

Gilberto goes shoulder-to-shoulder with Dortmund's giant Czech striker Jan Koller.

1 ARSENAL

Henry 18

1	David SEAMAN
12	LAUREN
23	Sol CAMPBELL
18	Pascal CYGAN
3	Ashley COLE
11	Sylvain WILTORD
4	Patrick VIEIRA
19	GILBERTO Silva
7	Robert PIRES
8	Fredrik LJUNGBERG
14	Thierry HENRY

Substitutes

13	Stuart TAYLOR
22	Oleg LUZHNY
26	Igors STEPANOVS
17	EDU (Gilberto) 80
28	Kolo TOURE (Pires) 67
25	Nwankwo KANU (Wiltord) 79
9	Francis JEFFERS

Lauren looks up and considers his options as a Dortmund player attempts to close him down.

bounced past Seaman via a post.

The second half brought more German pressure, though their winner proved controversial. After Koller won a race for possession with Seaman, the giant marksman tumbled dramatically and the referee awarded a penalty, which was converted emphatically by Rosicky.

Thereafter the Gunners rallied, and Ljungberg threatened in one penalty-box scramble, then set up Henry for a volley which flashed wide, but an equaliser never looked likely to materialise.

BOOKINGS

Borussia Dortmund Reuter 77

FA Barclaycard Premiership	30 October 2002						
	P	W	D	L	F	A	Pts
Liverpool	11	8	3	0	22	9	27
ARSENAL	11	7	2	2	26	13	23
Chelsea	11	5	4	2	20	12	19
Manchester United	11	5	4	2	14	8	19
Tottenham Hotspur	11	6	1	4	17	16	19
Middlesbrough	11	5	3	3	15	8	18
Blackburn Rovers	11	5	3	3	18	13	18
Everton	11	5	2	4	14	15	17
Newcastle United	10	5	1	4	16	15	16
Southampton	11	4	4	3	11	10	16
Fulham	11	4	3	4	16	14	15
Leeds United	11	4	2	5	13	12	14
Birmingham City	11	3	3	5	11	14	12
Aston Villa	11	3	2	6	7	11	11
West Ham United	11	3	2	6	10	17	11
Manchester City	11	3	2	6	9	17	11
Charlton Athletic	11	3	1	7	9	16	10
West Bromwich Albion	11	3	1	7	8	18	10
Sunderland	11	2	3	6	5	15	9
Bolton Wanderers	10	2	2	6	10	18	8

Pires and Vieira look on as Henry celebrates.

FA Barclaycard Premiership
Sunday 3 November 2002 at Loftus Road, 2 p.m.

FULHAM 0

1 Edwin VAN DER SAR

25 Abdeslam OUADDOU

4 Andy MELVILLE

24 Alain GOMA

3 Rufus BREVETT

2 Steve FINNAN

17 Martin DJETOU

18 Sylvain LEGWINSKI

14 Steed MALBRANQUE

11 Luis BOA MORTE

7 Steve MARLET

Substitutes

12 Maik TAYLOR

16 Zat KNIGHT

8 Lee CLARK

6 Junichi INAMOTO (Djetou) 54

15 Barry HAYLES (Malbranque) 54

Below *The luckless Steve Marlet slices his attempted clearance past Edwin van der Sar.*
Below, right *Sol Campbell and Edu celebrate while Henry looks on apologetically.*

MATCH REPORT

Arsenal's luck turned as they ended their run of four defeats with victory in a tense London derby and moved to within four points of table-topping Liverpool.

All that separated the two teams was a bizarre own goal from Marlet, whose wild swing at Henry's scuffed corner resulted in a wicked slice which left van der Sar helpless; and further to Fulham's chagrin, their concerted claims for two penalties fell on deaf ears.

That said, the Gunners fashioned the lion's share of clear scoring chances and produced several examples of free-flowing creative excellence that augured positively for the challenges ahead.

It was Fulham, though, who started the more convincingly, and they might have taken a first-minute lead when Malbranque's teasing cross eluded Cole and Finnan headed over from six yards.

Arsenal responded with a Ljungberg shot which cleared the crossbar, then came the first penalty appeal when Boa Morte rounded Cygan only to be flattened by Campbell. Soon afterwards Marlet might have done better with a header from a Finnan delivery and Campbell again escaped censure after felling Boa Morte.

But the Gunners looked devastating on the counter and van der Sar was forced to make two point-blank saves after Bergkamp had sent in first Henry, and then Ljungberg. Next, after

1 ARSENAL

Marlet og 31

1	David SEAMAN
12	LAUREN
23	Sol CAMPBELL
18	Pascal CYGAN
3	Ashley COLE
11	Sylvain WILTORD
19	GILBERTO Silva
17	EDU
8	Fredrik LJUNGBERG
10	Dennis BERGKAMP
14	Thierry HENRY

Substitutes

24	Rami SHAABAN
22	Oleg LUZHNY (Lauren) 65
7	Robert PIRES
28	Kolo TOURE (Wiltord) 83
25	Nwankwo KANU (Bergkamp) 72

BOOKINGS

Fulham Djetou 49
Arsenal Cygan 35, Edu 67

the visitors had gone in front, Wiltord executed an exquisite turn and lofted dink to set up Ljungberg, only for van der Sar to intervene again, blocking the Swede with his legs.

After the interval, Jean Tigana's side built up pressure, but Campbell and company stood admirably firm against their inventive opponents, and Seaman pulled off two splendid saves from the dangerous Legwinski, tipping over a firm header from a corner, then clutching a 20-yard drive at the second attempt. As the final whistle approached Arsenal returned to the offensive and the outstanding van der Sar prevented Henry from doubling the score from a narrow angle.

Top, left *Fredrik Ljungberg tangles with Rufus Brevett on the edge of the Fulham penalty area.*
Above, left *Gunners midfielders past (Junichi Inamoto) and present (Gilberto) clash.*

Worthington Cup, 3rd Round
Wednesday 6 November 2002 at Highbury, 8 p.m.

ARSENAL 2

Pires 12, Jeffers 32

13	Stuart TAYLOR
22	Oleg LUZHNY
26	Igors STEPANOVS
27	Stathis TAVLARIDIS
49	Sebastian SVARD
21	Jermaine PENNANT
7	Robert PIRES
16	Giovanni VAN BRONCKHORST
28	Kolo TOURE
25	Nwankwo KANU
9	Francis JEFFERS

Substitutes

24	Rami SHAABAN
40	Ryan GARRY (Svard) 81
29	Moritz VOLZ (Pennant) 81
45	Steven SIDWELL
47	Jerome THOMAS

Below *Francis Jeffers shoots past Jurgen Macho to give Arsenal a 2-0 lead.*
Below, right *Robert Pires celebrates with Giovanni van Bronckhorst.*

MATCH REPORT

The Gunners fell victim to a stunning fightback by Sunderland, who overturned a two-goal interval deficit with three headed strikes to reach the last 16 of the Worthington Cup.

In mitigation, Arsène Wenger had fielded what was virtually a second-string line-up, and they enjoyed no luck at all, but such reflections offered scant consolation for such a devastatingly unexpected reverse.

There had been no hint of trouble ahead as Arsenal had moved smoothly into a seemingly impregnable position, and it was particularly gratifying that their first goal was fashioned by two stars on the comeback trail from long-term injury. The creator was van Bronckhorst, who pulled back a low free-kick to Pires, enabling the Footballer of the Year to net with an unerring sidefoot from 20 yards.

Thereafter the hosts looked comfortable and they doubled their advantage when Kanu capped a determined run with a sumptuous curling delivery into the path of Jeffers, who jabbed the ball past Macho with the outside of his left foot. Soon after the

3 SUNDERLAND

Kyle 56, Stewart 70, Williams 72

30	Jurgen MACHO
34	Mark ROSSITER
6	Emerson THOME
22	Stanislav VARGA
27	George McCARTNEY
20	Stefan SCHWARZ
21	Paul THIRLWELL
18	Darren WILLIAMS
31	Marcus STEWART
19	Kevin KYLE
32	Michael PROCTOR

Substitutes

25	Ben CLARK
35	Clifford BYRNE
7	Matthew PIPER (Schwarz) 45
38	Craig TURNS
37	Johnjo DICKMAN

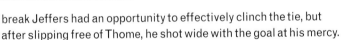

break Jeffers had an opportunity to effectively clinch the tie, but after slipping free of Thome, he shot wide with the goal at his mercy.

At the other end the most meaningful menace had materialised when Stepanovs almost slid the ball into his own net, but suddenly the contest was transformed as Stewart flicked on a Thirlwell corner and the untended Kyle headed home.

Now Sunderland had a whiff of salvation and, with the home rearguard looking increasingly vulnerable to aerial assault, Stewart met Proctor's cross from the right to nod an equaliser. Two minutes later the Wearsiders were ahead when Piper found space on the opposite flank and his dispatch was glanced past Taylor by Williams.

Now the Gunners rallied, launching wave after wave of attacks which forced the visitors to defend desperately, but both Jeffers and van Bronckhorst spurned chances to force extra time and Sunderland claimed their first victory at Highbury for 19 years.

BOOKINGS

Sunderland Piper 79

Above, left *Arsenal's 19-year-old Danish defender Sebastian Svard takes the fight to Sunderland's midfield.*

FA Barclaycard Premiership
Saturday 9 November 2002 at Highbury, 3 p.m.

ARSENAL 1

Wiltord 24

1	David SEAMAN
22	Oleg LUZHNY
23	Sol CAMPBELL
18	Pascal CYGAN
3	Ashley COLE
11	Sylvain WILTORD
19	GILBERTO Silva
4	Patrick VIEIRA
8	Fredrik LJUNGBERG
10	Dennis BERGKAMP
14	Thierry HENRY

Substitutes

13	Stuart TAYLOR
26	Igors STEPANOVS
17	EDU (Wiltord) 90
7	Robert PIRES (Bergkamp) 70
28	Kolo TOURE

Sylvain Wiltord meets Oleg Luzhny's measured cross with a sidefoot finish past Shay Given.

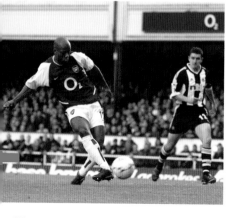

MATCH REPORT

The scoreline suggests a close contest, but it is misleading. In truth the Gunners, back to their irresistible best in every department except finishing, ripped the Magpies to shreds and might have won by an enormous margin.

Leading the charge was Henry, who set the tone after only three minutes when he sprinted through the centre of the Newcastle defence, then found Bergkamp on the left. The Dutchman stepped deftly inside a challenge, then dispatched a curler from 15 yards which bypassed Given but crashed against a post. The rebound found its way back to Bergkamp, but his follow-up was fielded by the Irish 'keeper.

As the traffic continued to roar in one direction, Vieira, who returned from suspension in awesome form, outjumped O'Brien from a corner only for his clean header to loop narrowly wide.

It seemed inconceivable that such dominance should remain unrewarded, and Arsenal duly took the lead in devastating fashion. Ljungberg delivered a majestic left-to-right crossfield ball to Henry, who tantalised two defenders, then touched on to the overlapping Luzhny, whose low cross was tapped in by the advancing Wiltord.

Soon Ljungberg almost extended the advantage when he raced on to a lofted pass from Vieira and lobbed over Given, only for the ball to land on the crossbar before bouncing clear. To this point there had been virtually no threat from Newcastle, but abruptly they burst into attacking life when Speed found Viana on the left and the Portuguese teenager smashed a sudden, savage drive against Seaman's bar.

0 NEWCASTLE UNITED

1	Shay GIVEN
12	Andy GRIFFIN
34	Nikos DABIZAS
5	Andy O'BRIEN
18	Aaron HUGHES
4	Nolberto SOLANO
7	Jermaine JENAS
11	Gary SPEED
45	Hugo VIANA
8	Kieron DYER
9	Alan SHEARER

Substitutes

13	Steve HARPER
35	Olivier BERNARD (Viana) 71
30	Stephen CALDWELL
23	Shola AMEOBI (Solano) 71
20	Lomana LUA-LUA

However, that was to prove an isolated incident as the hosts returned to the offensive. Given was forced into a point-blank block on Ljungberg and, shortly before the interval, Luzhny went close to his first Arsenal goal in nearly a century of appearances. The Gunners' command did not lessen in the second period, and though chances to Henry (twice) and Pires went begging, any other outcome but a home victory would have been a travesty.

BOOKINGS

Newcastle United Griffin 57, Viana 68

Above *Freddie Ljungberg takes on Newcastle's Nolberto Solano.*
Left *Gilberto controls the ball under pressure from Gary Speed and Jermaine Jenas.*

47

UEFA Champions League, Phase one, Group A
Tuesday 12 November 2002 at Highbury, 7.45 p.m.

ARSENAL 0

21	Rami SHAABAN
22	Oleg LUZHNY
26	Igors STEPANOVS
18	Pascal CYGAN
28	Kolo TOURE
7	Robert PIRES
4	Patrick VIEIRA
17	EDU
16	Giovanni VAN BRONCKHORST
14	Thierry HENRY
9	Francis JEFFERS

Substitutes

13	Stuart TAYLOR
3	Ashley COLE
27	Stathis TAVLARIDIS
8	Fredrik LJUNGBERG
19	GILBERTO Silva (Vieira) 77
10	Dennis BERGKAMP (Henry) 63
11	Sylvain WILTORD (Jeffers) 69

MATCH REPORT

Though Arsenal were disappointed to finish goalless for the first time in 32 matches, this less-than-riveting draw was enough for Arsène Wenger's men to top their qualifying group and ensure seeding for the second phase of the Champions League.

There were pluses, too, in a clean sheet on debut for 'keeper Shaaban and the continued rehabilitation following injury of Pires and van Bronckhorst. On the debit side was the dismissal of Toure for two bookable offences, which left the Gunners with ten men for the final hour.

Undeterred by the absence of a clutch of first-team regulars, Arsenal dominated the early exchanges. First Henry's deep cross found Jeffers, who nodded wide from ten yards; then Henry was off-target with a high chip and Jeffers' shot was blocked by the advancing Waterreus after the young Merseysider had been freed by a perceptive through-pass from Pires.

Shortly before half-time Ooijer appeared to fell Jeffers in the box but no penalty was awarded and, thus reprieved, PSV looked a more potent force thereafter. Indeed, only the legs of Shaaban prevented Kezman from converting a threaded delivery by van

Francis Jeffers sends a header narrowly wide of the PSV goal.

0   PSV EINDHOVEN

23	Ronald WATERREUS
30	Kasper BOGELUND
22	Wilfred BOUMA
3	Kevin HOFLAND
2	Andre OOIJER
19	Dennis ROMMEDAHL
6	Mark VAN BOMMEL
14	Johann VOGEL
11	Arjen ROBBEN
10	Arnold BRUGGINK
9	Mateja KEZMAN

Substitutes

1	Jelle TEN ROUWELAAR
4	Ernest FABER
5	Jan HEINTZE
16	Theo LUCIUS (Vogel) 41
13	Remco VAN DER SCHAAF
	(Bruggink) 71
7	Adil RAMZI
8	Jan VENNEGOOR of HESSELINK
	(Ooijer) 80

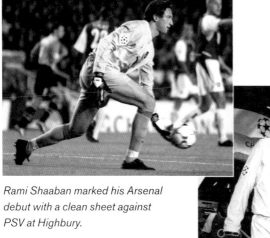

Rami Shaaban marked his Arsenal debut with a clean sheet against PSV at Highbury.

BOOKINGS

Arsenal Toure 29
PSV Eindhoven Vogel 24, Ooijer 45, Hofland 65, Hesselink 90, van Bommel 90

DISMISSALS

Arsenal Toure 35

Bommel and Robben fired marginally high after a mazy run.

The introduction of Bergkamp and Wiltord from the bench renewed the Gunners' impetus, however. The Dutchman was close to connecting with a pull-back from Pires, then a dazzling combination between the two reinforcements climaxed with Wiltord firing across goal and narrowly wide of the far post.

The Frenchman went close once more before late PSV pressure almost produced a goal when a misdirected clearance following a van Bommel corner landed on Shaaban's crossbar. Finally Waterreus, who had joined his attack in desperation, failed to connect with a header and the draw was secured.

49

FA Barclaycard Premiership
Saturday 16 November 2002 at Highbury, 3 p.m.

ARSENAL 3

Henry 13, Ljungberg 55, Wiltord 71

24	Rami SHAABAN
22	Oleg LUZHNY
23	Sol CAMPBELL
18	Pascal CYGAN
3	Ashley COLE
11	Sylvain WILTORD
19	GILBERTO Silva
4	Patrick VIEIRA
8	Fredrik LJUNGBERG
10	Dennis BERGKAMP
14	Thierry HENRY

Substitutes

13	Stuart TAYLOR
16	Giovanni VAN BRONCKHORST
	(Vieira) 78
28	Kolo TOURE
7	Robert PIRES (Bergkamp) 26
9	Francis JEFFERS (Henry) 75

Thierry Henry en route to scoring The Premiership's Goal of the Season.

MATCH REPORT

Tottenham were ruthlessly swept aside as the Gunners reclaimed the Premiership top spot for the first time in six weeks with a glittering display which featured a goal of world-class quality.

Latching on to a Vieira clearance not far outside Arsenal's penalty box, Henry set off on a jinking 70-yard dash which took him past Etherington, Carr and King before he buried a venomous low drive from 16 yards.

By then the visitors, seeking their first Highbury victory in nearly a decade, were already on the back foot, trapped there by wave upon relentless wave of bewilderingly fluent attacks.

Even before the Henry masterpiece, Gilberto had brought a smart save from Keller, and Wiltord might have plundered a hat-trick, seeing one effort disallowed for offside, another blocked by King and a third creep narrowly wide. Meanwhile at the other end, Shaaban's competent fielding of a Redknapp 25-yarder was the only significant action.

True, Keane might have delivered a prompt equaliser but his header from a searching Davies cross was tame, and soon Spurs' afternoon took another turn for the worse when the Welshman was the victim of a harsh dismissal for a second bookable offence.

Before the break Henry netted again, only to be ruled offside, but there

0   TOTTENHAM HOTSPUR

13	Kasey KELLER
2	Stephen CARR
26	Ledley KING
36	Dean RICHARDS
5	Goran BUNJEVCEVIC
29	Simon DAVIES
4	Steffen FREUND
15	Jamie REDKNAPP
28	Matthew ETHERINGTON
10	Teddy SHERINGHAM
22	Robbie KEANE

Substitutes

24	Lars HIRSCHFIELD
6	Chris PERRY
7	Darren ANDERTON (Redknapp) 65
14	Gustavo POYET (Etherington) 45
16	Steffen IVERSEN (Sheringham) 64

BOOKINGS

Tottenham Hotspur Davies 23,
Poyet 49

DISMISSALS

Tottenham Hotspur Davies 27

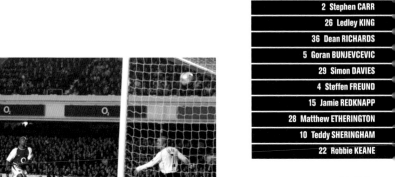

was no denying the Champions, who went further ahead when Ljungberg combined neatly with Wiltord and Henry before sidefooting home from eight yards.

In response, Poyet sent Richards through on goal but his dink past Shaaban was retrieved by Cygan, who then freed Pires for an exquisite chip that landed on top of the net.

Arsenal added a third goal when Keller blocked Henry's shot and the ball rebounded to Pires, whose sweet diagonal pass was converted fiercely by Wiltord.

Shaaban completed his League debut by fisting away a ferocious free-kick by Anderton, but that was merely an isolated gesture of defiance by a well-beaten side.

Above, left *Sylvain Wiltord watches his powerful shot fly into the corner of the Spurs net despite the efforts of defender Stephen Carr on the line.*

SOUTHAMPTON 3

Beattie 45, 59 pen, Delgado 67

14	Antti NIEMI
2	Jason DODD
5	Claus LUNDEKVAM
11	Michael SVENSSON
3	Wayne BRIDGE
18	Rory DELAP
4	Chris MARSDEN
8	Matt OAKLEY
29	Fabrice FERNANDES
9	James BEATTIE
34	AGUSTIN DELGADO

Substitutes

1	Paul JONES
6	Paul WILLIAMS
12	Anders SVENSSON
33	Paul TELFER (Fernandes) 87
36	Brett ORMEROD (Delgado) 83

Edu puts a celebratory arm around goalscorer Dennis Bergkamp.

MATCH REPORT

A desperate late comeback bid by ten-man Arsenal failed to prevent their third defeat of the Premiership campaign.

The outcome was particularly frustrating for the Gunners in that they had taken a first-half lead with a brilliant Bergkamp goal, then were denied further joy by the heroics of Southampton 'keeper Niemi. That said, the Saints created a stack of scoring opportunities, too, and it required a splendid display by Seaman to keep them within reach.

Passing smoothly from the outset, Arsenal almost snatched an early initiative but Luzhny's cross was glanced wide by Henry. Southampton retaliated with an Oakley snap-shot which demanded a sprawling save from Seaman, but then the visitors' fluency paid dividends when a sweeping move culminated in Bergkamp half-volleying sweetly past Niemi from 20 yards.

Southampton equalised on the stroke of half-time when Cygan fouled Delgado and, from the resultant free-kick, Beattie drilled just inside a post.

Shortly after the break Vieira seemed certain to restore Arsenal's advantage but he was denied by three fabulous blocks in the space of ten seconds by Niemi, and then the balance of power shifted.

A Cygan slip allowed Delgado to run free and the Ecuadorian was downed by Campbell's honest attempt to win the ball. However, the England man was dismissed, Beattie sent Seaman the wrong way from the

2 ARSENAL

Bergkamp 36, Pires 80

1	David SEAMAN
22	Oleg LUZHNY
23	Sol CAMPBELL
18	Pascal CYGAN
3	Ashley COLE
11	Sylvain WILTORD
4	Patrick VIEIRA
17	EDU
8	Fredrik LJUNGBERG
10	Dennis BERGKAMP
14	Thierry HENRY

Substitutes

13	Stuart TAYLOR
28	Kolo TOURE (Edu) 61
19	GILBERTO Silva
7	Robert PIRES (Bergkamp) 73
9	Francis JEFFERS (Ljungberg) 72

spot and soon the Gunners' plight deteriorated further when Delgado bundled in at the far post following a Fernandes free-kick.

They might have been buried altogether, but Delap missed with a header, then Seaman made two smart saves from Beattie, after which Arsenal rallied bravely. Niemi beat out a scorcher from Henry, but although he parried a Pires header he could not repel the Frenchman's close-range follow-up and the fight was on.

Thereafter, though, the nearest the Champions came to rescuing a point was when Henry almost intercepted a loose back-pass from Marsden.

BOOKINGS

Southampton Marsden 70
Arsenal Cole 60, Vieira 90

DISMISSALS

Arsenal Campbell 57

Top left *Thierry Henry out-muscles Southampton's Jason Dodd.*

Left *Too little too late… Robert Pires scores in the 80th minute as Kolo Toure looks on.*

53

ROMA 1

Cassano 4

1 Francesco ANTONIOLI
5 Jonathan ZEBINA
19 Walter SAMUEL
23 Christian PANUCCI
2 Marcus CAFU
11 Fereira EMERSON
8 Francisco LIMA
32 Vincent CANDELA
10 Francesco TOTTI
18 Antonio CASSANO
24 Marco DELVECCHIO

Substitutes

22 Ivan PELIZZOLI
13 Leandro CUFRE
20 Davide BOMBARDINI
28 Josep GUARDIOLA
25 Gianni GUIGOU (Delvecchio) 57
9 Vincenzo MONTELLA (Cassano) 64
33 Gabriel BATISTUTA (Lima) 73

MATCH REPORT

A scintillating hat-trick by Thierry Henry swept Arsenal to a glorious victory over shell-shocked Roma. The Frenchman's world-class display represented a devastatingly ruthless riposte after the Gunners had been rocked by conceding an early goal.

The game began at a fierce tempo with Cygan lunging desperately to foil Cassano, but the lively youngster bounced back almost instantly with the opening score. After exchanging passes with Totti on the left, he stepped inside Campbell, then scuffed a shot which hit Shaaban's near upright before spinning along the line and into the net at the far post.

The Arsenal response was both swift and deadly, Gilberto holding off two challenges to dispatch a crossfield pass to Henry, who curled home with precision from the edge of the box.

Roma almost regained their lead when Cafu's floated cross was controlled superbly by Totti and volleyed goalwards from eight yards, but Cygan was the saviour with an heroic clearance off the line.

Gilberto missed narrowly with a downward header shortly before the break, but Arsenal had an escape of their own after 64 minutes when Shaaban felled the charging Guigou but no penalty was given.

That proved a crucial decision, as Henry seized control with two goals in five minutes. When Luzhny delivered a long, raking cross

The 'Thierry Henry Show' gets under way as the Frenchman curls home Arsenal's opening goal after just six minutes.

3 ARSENAL

Henry 6, 70, 75

from the right, the Frenchman's header rebounded conveniently from the back of Panucci and he netted emphatically from eight yards.

Then, with Roma still reeling, Wiltord was fouled by Emerson near the left angle of the area, and Henry curled an unstoppable dipping free-kick past the rooted Antonioli. It was a goal fit to settle any contest, all the more satisfying as it capped a confident and coherent all-round performance.

24	Rami SHAABAN
22	Oleg LUZHNY
23	Sol CAMPBELL
18	Pascal CYGAN
3	Ashley COLE
7	Robert PIRES
19	GILBERTO Silva
4	Patrick VIEIRA
8	Fredrik LJUNGBERG
11	Sylvain WILTORD
14	Thierry HENRY

Substitutes

13	Stuart TAYLOR
5	Martin KEOWN (Wiltord) 84
26	Igors STEPANOVS
29	Moritz VOLZ
17	EDU (Ljungberg) 90
16	Giovanni VAN BRONCKHORST
	(Pires) 78
9	Francis JEFFERS

BOOKINGS

Roma Samuel 41, Emerson 74, Batistuta 80

Above *Henry completes a memorable hat-trick with an unstoppable free-kick from the edge of the penalty area.*
Right *Wiltord, Cygan and Keown applaud the travelling Gunners fans.*

ARSENAL 3

Pires 17, Henry 49, 82 pen

24	Rami SHAABAN
22	Oleg LUZHNY
23	Sol CAMPBELL
18	Pascal CYGAN
16	Giovanni VAN BRONCKHORST
28	Kolo TOURE
19	GILBERTO Silva
4	Patrick VIEIRA
7	Robert PIRES
10	Dennis BERGKAMP
14	Thierry HENRY

Substitutes

13	Stuart TAYLOR
5	Martin KEOWN (Toure) 67
8	Fredrik LJUNGBERG (Pires) 71
11	Sylvain WILTORD (Bergkamp) 71
9	Francis JEFFERS

MATCH REPORT

The Gunners stretched their Premiership lead to four points with yet another exhibition of delightful attacking football, marred only slightly by a second-half period of defensive uncertainty when Villa threatened to salvage a draw.

The Champions began in typical style, with Vieira and Bergkamp combining sweetly to find Toure, whose rasping drive was repelled acrobatically by Enckelman.

Vassell fired a warning shot across Arsenal bows when he nipped past Campbell and forced Shaaban into a low save, but the hosts took the lead when Bergkamp seized on a loose ball and freed Pires to net clinically from the edge of the area.

At this point, it seemed, Villa were there for the taking, but Arsenal could not find a way past Enckelman. Pires missed the ball altogether when set up by Henry, then Toure tapped home after Henry had shot against a post, only for the linesman to raise a contentious offside flag.

After that, Bergkamp scuffed uncharacteristically following a Pires run, but shortly before the interval Villa showed signs of retaliation, with Leonhardsen and Dublin going close.

However, Arsenal made a perfect start to the second period, Henry curling in a sumptuous free-kick from the left corner of the box, a replica of his effort in Rome three days earlier.

But the visitors remained unbowed and Hitzlsperger set up a hugely entertaining if unexpectedly anxious final half-hour with an

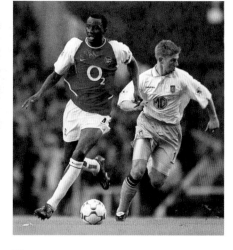

Gunners skipper Patrick Vieira strides forward with Villa's Tomas Hitzlsperger in hot pursuit.

1 ASTON VILLA

Hitzlsperger 64

1	Peter ENCKELMAN
4	Olof MELLBERG
27	Ronny JOHNSEN
11	Steve STAUNTON
21	J Lloyd SAMUEL
17	Lee HENDRIE
12	Tomas HITZLSPERGER
7	Ian TAYLOR
28	Oyvind LEONHARDSEN
9	Dion DUBLIN
10	Darius VASSELL

Substitutes

13	Stefan POSTMA
15	Ulises DE LA CRUZ (Hendrie) 45
26	Mark KINSELLA
14	Marcus ALLBACK
8	Juan Pablo ANGEL

explosive cross-shot which ripped into the far top corner of the Arsenal net.

Sensing the possibility of reward, Villa attacked with enterprise and De La Cruz saw one powerful effort blocked and the follow-up repelled smartly by Shaaban.

Thus there was a collective sigh of relief around Highbury when Staunton was adjudged to have fouled Ljungberg inside the box and Henry stepped up to dink a cheeky spot-kick into the centre of the diving Enckelman's net.

Robert Pires drives home the opening goal.

FA Barclaycard Premiership	30 November 2002						
	P	W	D	L	F	A	Pts
ARSENAL	16	11	2	3	36	17	35
Liverpool	15	9	4	2	26	13	31
Chelsea	16	8	6	2	28	13	30
Everton	15	9	2	4	18	15	29
Manchester United	15	7	5	3	23	16	26
Middlesbrough	16	7	3	6	19	13	24
Tottenham Hotspur	16	7	3	6	20	22	24
Blackburn Rovers	16	6	5	5	22	19	23
Newcastle United	14	7	1	6	23	22	22
Southampton	15	5	5	5	17	17	20
Birmingham City	16	5	5	6	16	19	20
Manchester City	16	6	2	8	17	23	20
Fulham	16	5	4	7	21	22	19
Aston Villa	16	5	4	7	15	16	19
Leeds United	15	5	2	8	19	22	17
Charlton Athletic	15	5	2	8	14	19	17
West Bromwich Albion	16	4	3	9	11	22	15
Sunderland	16	3	5	8	8	20	14
Bolton Wanderers	15	3	4	8	17	27	13
West Ham United	15	3	3	9	15	28	12

Thierry Henry scores with a glorious, curling free-kick to make it 2-0.

57

MANCHESTER UNITED 2
Veron 22, Scholes 72

1 Fabien BARTHEZ
2 Gary NEVILLE
24 Wesley BROWN
27 Mikael SILVESTRE
22 John O'SHEA
20 Ole Gunnar SOLSKJAER
4 Juan Sebastian VERON
3 Phil NEVILLE
11 Ryan GIGGS
18 Paul SCHOLES
10 Ruud VAN NISTELROOY

Substitutes
19 RICARDO
14 David MAY
17 Michael STEWART
15 Luke CHADWICK
21 Diego FORLAN

MATCH REPORT

The last time the Gunners called at Old Trafford, they left with the Premiership crown in their keeping; this time they were beaten soundly. It was a defeat that left United just three points behind the Champions, although it's fair to observe that not a single break went Arsenal's way.

Van Nistelrooy was palpably guilty of handball in the move which led to United's first goal, Scholes' shot for their second was deflected off Keown and Arsenal's best effort, a sublime chip by Pires after the sweetest of interplay with Henry, shaved the frame of the goal.

That said, the Red Devils deserved their victory because of their insatiable desire, which condemned Arsène Wenger's team to their first blank scoresheet in 56 Premiership outings and, more seriously, a fourth defeat in eight League matches.

After weathering a whirlwind start from their hosts, the Gunners threatened briefly to seize the initiative. Gary Neville stepped under a Luzhny cross to leave Henry through on goal, only for Barthez to gather his countryman's sidefooted shot, then came the link between Henry and Pires which was thwarted so agonisingly when Barthez got his fingertips to the arcing delivery.

That impetus was quelled cruelly when van Nistelrooy controlled with

Freddie Ljungberg bears down on goal under pressure from Giggs.

0 ARSENAL

24	Rami SHAABAN
22	Oleg LUZHNY
5	Martin KEOWN
18	Pascal CYGAN
3	Ashley COLE
8	Fredrik LJUNGBERG
19	GILBERTO Silva
4	Patrick VIEIRA
7	Robert PIRES
11	Sylvain WILTORD
14	Thierry HENRY

Substitutes

13	Stuart TAYLOR (Shaaban) 43
12	LAUREN
16	Giovanni VAN BRONCKHORST
28	Kolo TOURE (Pires) 76
10	Dennis BERGKAMP (Wiltord) 67

his hand and switched to Scholes, whose low, driven cross was tapped in by the untended Veron.

Henry netted in first-half stoppage time only for the strike to be disallowed for a foul on Phil Neville, but after Taylor had blocked a Giggs half-volley at point-blank range, Arsenal upped the tempo and might have scored twice. A Pires corner reached Cygan, but his fierce drive was repelled by O'Shea, then Luzhny found Gilberto, who sliced wide of the near post.

Soon afterwards the Gunners were undone when van Nistelrooy tricked Cygan on the right and rolled a pass inside to Scholes, who side-stepped Keown before flashing home a powerful ten-yard drive via the recovering defender's boot.

All that remained was a free-kick from Henry which flew wide, summing up a day when little went right for Arsenal.

BOOKINGS

Manchester United P Neville 79
Arsenal Luzhny 82, Toure 86

Top *Patrick Vieira races to collect a loose ball.*
Bottom *The unlucky Rami Shaaban holds the injured thigh that forced him out of the action just before half time.*

ARSENAL 0

1	David SEAMAN
12	LAUREN
23	Sol CAMPBELL
18	Pascal CYGAN
3	Ashley COLE
8	Fredrik LJUNGBERG
19	GILBERTO Silva
4	Patrick VIEIRA
7	Robert PIRES
10	Dennis BERGKAMP
14	Thierry HENRY

Substitutes

13	Stuart TAYLOR
5	Martin KEOWN
22	Oleg LUZHNY
17	EDU
15	Ray PARLOUR (Vieira) 38
25	Nwankwo KANU (Pires) 83
11	Sylvain WILTORD (Ljungberg) 78

MATCH REPORT

Most of the thrills from a frustrating yet fitfully fascinating encounter between the Champions of England and Spain were crammed into the dying minutes, when both sides went close to breaking the deadlock.

It was a story of steady if uncharacteristically uninspired Arsenal pressure in the face of well-drilled resistance from the skilful, belligerent visitors, and it appeared to be drawing to an uneventful close when the ball fell to Kanu after Ayala had failed to deal with a high cross.

The Nigerian hammered a shot goalwards only to be foiled by the splendid Palop and although the rebound presented Wiltord with an even more inviting opportunity, the Frenchman scuffed his effort, allowing Marchena to clear off the line.

Suddenly the action switched to the opposite end where Carew scooped a Rufete dispatch over the stranded Seaman but the Gunners were saved by Campbell, who hacked the ball to safety.

All that late drama was unrepresentative of what had gone before, although Arsène Wenger's men had fashioned enough scoring openings to have claimed all three points.

Dennis Bergkamp holds off the challenge of Roberto Ayala.

0 VALENCIA

13	Andres PALOP
15	Amedeo CARBONI
2	Mauricio PELLEGRINO
4	Roberto AYALA
23	Cristobal CURRO TORRES
10	Miguel ANGULO
8	Ruben BARAJA
6	David ALBELDA
14	Rodrigues VICENTE
21	Pablo AIMAR
7	John CAREW

Bergkamp was the man behind the two best first-half moments, surging down the left to deliver a cross which only just eluded Ljungberg, then flicking cutely to Vieira, who sent in Henry only for Palop to block the Frenchman's tame shot.

The Valencia 'keeper excelled after the interval, too, catching a firm header from Bergkamp and blocking Ljungberg at close range when the Swede turned sweetly on to a Pires pass.

Soon after that the Spaniards were reduced to ten men when Angulo was red-carded for swiping Cygan in the stomach, and their only attacking threat came from the pace of Carew, who failed to get a shot on target.

Arsenal were disappointed at the final whistle, but the point was enough to leave them on top of their group on goal difference as they entered the Champions League winter break.

Valencia 'keeper Andres Palop spreads himself to block a late shot from Kanu.

Substitutes

25	David RANGEL
3	Fabio AURELIO (Baraja) 87
24	Javier GARRIDO
12	Carlos MARCHENA (Aimar) 79
22	Gonzalo DE LOS SANTOS
19	Francisco RUFETE (Vicente) 68
11	Juan SANCHEZ

DISMISSALS

Valencia Angulo 72

FA Barclaycard Premiership
Sunday 15 December 2002 at White Hart Lane, 2 p.m.

TOTTENHAM HOTSPUR   1

Ziege 11

13 Kasey KELLER
26 Ledley KING
36 Dean RICHARDS
5 Goran BUNJEVCEVIC
2 Stephen CARR
23 Christian ZIEGE
4 Steffen FREUND
7 Darren ANDERTON
14 Gustavo POYET
10 Teddy SHERINGHAM
22 Robbie KEANE

Substitutes

24 Lars HIRSCHFIELD
6 Chris PERRY
25 Stephen CLEMENCE
29 Simon DAVIES (Anderton) 71
16 Steffen IVERSEN

MATCH REPORT

Arsenal clawed their way back from the brink of meltdown in the North London derby to salvage a point in the manner of true Champions. For most of the first period the Gunners were dominated comprehensively by a pumped-up Spurs side, who struck one remarkable goal and might have added several more before Arsène Wenger's men snatched an equaliser on the stroke of half-time.

Thereafter Arsenal rallied, holding their own throughout the second 45 minutes and even creating several chances to sneak a victory themselves.

Tottenham began at a furious tempo and Seaman had already been at full stretch to clear from Ziege when he was beaten by a thunderous 33-yard free-kick from the German after Campbell had fouled Poyet.

Three minutes later the lead might have been doubled by Keane's header from an Anderton corner but Cole made the first of two sensational goal-line clearances, the second coming from a scorching Keane drive.

In between Arsenal had threatened briefly through a Parlour 30-yarder which demanded a smart save from Keller, and Gilberto nodded wide, but the impetus remained with Tottenham and Seaman made a succession of timely interventions.

However, shortly after Keller had repelled a fine diving header from Henry, the balance of power shifted. The Frenchman was chasing a seemingly harmless loose ball when Keller charged from his line and brought him down. Pires converted the

Thierry Henry stretches to reach the ball ahead of Spurs' Ledley King.

1 ARSENAL

Pires 44 pen

penalty coolly and the Gunners were back in contention.
Having roused themselves from their first-half torpor,
the visitors were a far more formidable proposition
after the interval, and Henry brought the crowd to
its feet with a thrilling 50-yard dribble past three
defenders which climaxed in a pass to Bergkamp,
whose shot was blocked.

Spurs hit back and Seaman made two more outstanding saves from Keane, then Sheringham
was off-target with a last-minute header. But
Arsenal clung on; certainly a case of one
point gained rather than two lost.

1	David SEAMAN
12	LAUREN
23	Sol CAMPBELL
5	Martin KEOWN
3	Ashley COLE
8	Fredrik LJUNGBERG
19	GILBERTO Silva
5	Ray PARLOUR
7	Robert PIRES
10	Dennis BERGKAMP
14	Thierry HENRY

Substitutes

13	Stuart TAYLOR
20	Matthew UPSON
16	Giovanni VAN BRONCKHORST
	(Pires) 80
28	Kolo TOURE (Ljungberg) 87
11	Sylvain WILTORD (Bergkamp) 71

BOOKINGS

Tottenham Hotspur Keller 44,
Sheringham 63, Freund 73
Arsenal Lauren 82, Parlour 89

*Robert Pires takes
responsibility and fires
home Arsenal's
equaliser from the
penalty spot.*

63

FA Barclaycard Premiership
Saturday 21 December 2002 at Highbury, 3 p.m.

ARSENAL 2

Campbell 45, Pires 90

1	David SEAMAN
12	LAUREN
5	Martin KEOWN
23	Sol CAMPBELL
3	Ashley COLE
11	Sylvain WILTORD
19	GILBERTO Silva
16	Giovanni VAN BRONCKHORST
8	Fredrik LJUNGBERG
7	Robert PIRES
14	Thierry HENRY

Substitutes

24	Rami SHAABAN
22	Oleg LUZHNY
28	Kolo TOURE
25	Nwankwo KANU
9	Francis JEFFERS

*Sol Campbell celebrates
his brave headed goal that
gave Arsenal a deserved
interval lead.*

MATCH REPORT

A hard-earned victory over tenacious if distinctly unenterprising opponents ensured that the Gunners would spend Christmas on top of the Premiership tree for the first time in their history.

Though never at their fluent best, Arsène Wenger's team created enough scoring opportunities to have triumphed comfortably, rather than relying on strikes in stoppage time at the end of each half.

They began purposefully, with Pires feeding van Bronckhorst – an emergency replacement for Parlour, who was injured in the warm-up – but the Dutchman's powerful drive flashed past a post.

A Wiltord 20-yarder was deflected marginally high, then Campbell's nod from a Pires corner grazed a post on the way to safety as the pressure built and Middlesbrough offered little by way of attacking retaliation.

Arsenal deserved an interval lead, which they secured when van Bronckhorst delivered a swirling free-kick from the left and Campbell, disregarding the outstretched boot of England colleague Southgate, launched himself to net with a courageous header.

0 MIDDLESBROUGH

1	Mark SCHWARZER
30	STUART PARNABY
4	Ugo EHIOGU
6	Gareth SOUTHGATE
3	Frank QUEUDRUE
12	Jonathan GREENING
14	GEREMI
7	George BOATENG
31	Luke WILKSHIRE
8	Szilard NEMETH
11	Alen BOKSIC

Substitutes

25	Mark CROSSLEY
15	Tony VIDMAR (Nemeth) 78
10	Josephe-Desire JOB (Boateng) 25
20	Dean WINDASS (Boksic) 70
9	Massimo MACCARONE

The hosts began the second half at breakneck speed and almost doubled their lead when a delicious Pires flick freed Wiltord on the right, only for Henry to miskick from his fellow Frenchman's inviting cross.

A Geremi drive which cleared Seaman's bar offered an isolated threat from Middlesbrough, but most of the action was at the other end where Wilkshire, soon to be dismissed for a second bookable offence, cleared off his goal-line from Gilberto.

By now Schwarzer was the busiest man on the field, and he pulled off two spendid saves, first repelling a Wiltord cross-shot after fine work from Cole and Pires, then tipping an acrobatic volley from Henry on to a post.

Yet for all the Gunners' command, it looked as though a second goal would elude them until Henry broke free on the left and fired a crossfield pass to Pires, which enabled the Footballer of the Year to net with a low drive into the far corner of Schwarzer's net.

BOOKINGS

Arsenal Cole 30
Middlesbrough Greening 42,
Wilkshire 44, Queudrue 86

DISMISSALS

Middlesbrough Wilkshire 73

Top *Boro's Frank Queudrue takes a firm hold of Gio van Bronckhorst's shirt.*
Bottom *Robert Pires scores Arsenal's second goal with an accurate 90th-minute drive.*

65

WEST BROMWICH ALBION 1

Dichio 3

1 Russell HOULT
17 Larus SIGURDSSON
5 Darren MOORE
14 Sean GREGAN
23 Adam CHAMBERS
18 Jason KOUMAS
7 Ronnie WALLWORK
10 Andy JOHNSON
3 Neil CLEMENT
9 Daniele DICHIO
11 Jason ROBERTS

Substitutes

31 Joe MURPHY
2 Igor BALIS
22 James CHAMBERS (Wallwork) 84
12 Scott DOBIE (A Chambers) 85
19 Lee HUGHES

MATCH REPORT

Arsenal showed the resilience and quality demanded of Champions as they stretched their advantage at the Premiership summit to four points, thanks to a late winner against the lowly but indomitably valiant Baggies.

Albion attacked from the first whistle and soon Dichio had Seaman stretching to tip over a sweetly struck 25-yarder. Then, with the Gunners' rearguard still reeling from the ferocity of the onslaught, Koumas swung over a corner and Dichio rose to net with a thunderous header from six yards.

Thus forced on to the back foot, the visitors spent the rest of the first half in battling for a foothold against their feisty opponents, and they were sustained by an inspirational display from their skipper Vieira, whose tackling, chasing and passing were a wonder to behold.

Russell Hoult flails helplessly as Francis Jeffers' goalbound shot slips past him.

2 ARSENAL

Jeffers 48, Henry 85

1	David SEAMAN
12	LAUREN
23	Sol CAMPBELL
5	Martin KEOWN
3	Ashley COLE
11	Sylvain WILTORD
19	GILBERTO Silva
4	Patrick VIEIRA
16	Giovanni VAN BRONCKHORST
9	Francis JEFFERS
14	Thierry HENRY

Substitutes

41	Craig HOLLOWAY
20	Matthew UPSON
28	Kolo TOURE
7	Robert PIRES (van Bronckhorst) 69
25	Nwankwo KANU (Jeffers) 69

The only notable threat from Arsenal before the interval was a miscued cross from Wiltord which almost crept under Hoult's bar, but they made a potent start to the second when Henry ran on to Gilberto's crossfield dispatch and backheeled to van Bronckhorst, whose cross-shot forced an agile save from the Albion 'keeper.

The tenor of the contest had changed and shortly afterwards the Gunners levelled when Henry's low delivery from the left was deflected into the path of Jeffers, who squeezed his shot past Hoult from five yards.

Albion were not lying down, however, and Sigurdsson nodded narrowly wide from a Koumas free-kick, then Moore's long pass reached Roberts, who sidestepped Keown and fired past Seaman, only for his effort to rebound to safety from the base of a post.

Arsenal, too, were creating openings, first for Henry, who scooped high from 12 yards, then for Pires, who nodded a Cole cross past an upright.

Finally, with six minutes remaining, Vieira charged down a Chambers clearance, Henry's superb first touch took him around Hoult, and his second slotted the ball into the empty net.

BOOKINGS

West Bromwich Albion Dichio 36

Patrick Vieira controls the ball under the watchful eye of Andy Johnson.

Thierry Henry's 85th-minute shot loops in despite the efforts of Hoult.

FA Barclaycard Premiership
Sunday 29 December 2002 at Highbury, 4 p.m.

ARSENAL 1
Henry 79 pen

1 David SEAMAN
12 LAUREN
23 Sol CAMPBELL
5 Martin KEOWN
3 Ashley COLE
11 Sylvain WILTORD
19 GILBERTO Silva
4 Patrick VIEIRA
7 Robert PIRES
25 Nwankwo KANU
14 Thierry HENRY

Substitutes

13 Stuart TAYLOR
22 Oleg LUZHNY
16 Giovanni VAN BRONCKHORST
(Pires) 84
10 Dennis BERGKAMP (Kanu) 65
9 Francis JEFFERS (Wiltord) 77

Liverpool's John Arne Riise puts an ill-advised arm across Francis Jeffers and gives away the 79th-minute that led to Arsenal's equaliser.

MATCH REPORT

The Gunners came from behind to snatch a precious point in a game of two penalties, and almost grabbed a sensational winner through Gilberto in the fourth minute of stoppage time.

In truth, a draw was a fair outcome to a contest in which Arsenal had dominated first-half possession without capitalising on their superiority but Liverpool, who were looking for their first win in nine Premiership outings, fought back spiritedly after the break.

Both sides started tentatively, but after Seaman held a low 25-yarder from Riise, the hosts assumed territorial command. A Vieira scorcher was blocked by Riise, then Campbell netted with a header from a Henry corner, only to be penalised for fouling Diao.

But Liverpool defended doggedly, restricting Arsenal's first-half openings to an incursion by Wiltord, which was ended by Kirkland's courageous dive at the Frenchman's feet, and headers from Henry and Campbell, which flew wide.

The visitors began the second period more adventurously and initially the Gunners revelled in the resulting space. Kirkland spilled a deflected Henry drive, then brilliantly fingertipped Pires' follow-up over the bar, and Wiltord skipped past Carragher but missed the target.

At last Liverpool materialised as an attacking force, and Diouf miscued horribly with a three-yard header which was cleared by Cole, then a Seaman fumble allowed Baros to shoot against the post from a narrow angle.

The deadlock was broken when a raking delivery from Gerrard found Baros, who was felled in the box by Campbell and

1 LIVERPOOL

Murphy 69 pen

22	Chris KIRKLAND
23	Jamie CARRAGHER
4	Sami HYYPIA
2	Stephane HENCHOZ
18	John Arne RIISE
13	Danny MURPHY
17	Steven GERRARD
21	Salif DIAO
28	Bruno CHEYROU
5	Milan BAROS
10	Michael OWEN

Substitutes

19	Pegguy ARPHEXAD
30	Djimi TRAORE (Cheyrou) 80
25	Igor BISCAN (Baros) 86
9	El Hadji DIOUF (Owen) 33
33.	Neil MELLOR

Murphy netted coolly from the spot.

Ten minutes later Arsenal were level when Bergkamp picked out Jeffers, who turned sweetly past Riise and sprawled headlong. The referee awarded a controversial penalty, which was converted emphatically by Henry.

Now the Gunners looked the likelier winners and might have claimed victory in the dying seconds when Bergkamp located Cole, who stabbed a pass across the six-yard box, only for Gilberto to sidefoot inches wide.

BOOKINGS

Arsenal Campbell 73
Liverpool Diao 35, Murphy 50, Riise 79

FA Barclaycard Premiership	29 December 2002						
	P	W	D	L	F	A	Pts
ARSENAL	21	13	4	4	42	22	43
Chelsea	21	10	8	3	34	17	38
Manchester United	21	11	5	5	33	21	38
Newcastle United	20	11	2	7	34	29	35
Everton	21	10	5	6	23	22	35
Liverpool	21	9	7	5	30	21	34
Southampton	21	8	8	5	24	20	32
Tottenham Hotspur	21	9	5	7	30	30	32
Manchester City	21	9	3	9	28	29	30
Middlesbrough	21	8	5	8	25	20	29
Blackburn Rovers	21	7	8	6	28	25	29
Charlton Athletic	21	8	5	8	24	25	29
Leeds United	21	8	3	10	28	27	27
Aston Villa	21	7	4	10	19	23	25
Birmingham City	21	6	7	8	19	25	25
Fulham	21	6	5	10	23	27	23
Bolton Wanderers	20	4	7	9	23	35	19
Sunderland	21	4	6	11	14	30	18
West Bromwich Albion	21	4	4	13	16	32	16
West Ham United	21	3	7	11	21	38	16

Above *Thierry Henry crashes home Arsenal's equaliser with an emphatically taken penalty.*

ARSENAL 3

Desailly og 9, van Bronckhorst 81, Henry 82

1 David SEAMAN
22 Oleg LUZHNY
23 Sol CAMPBELL
5 Martin KEOWN
3 Ashley COLE
11 Sylvain WILTORD
19 GILBERTO Silva
4 Patrick VIEIRA
7 Robert PIRES
10 Dennis BERGKAMP
14 Thierry HENRY

Substitutes

13 Stuart TAYLOR
12 LAUREN (Wiltord) 69
28 Kolo TOURE (Bergkamp) 79
16 Giovanni VAN BRONCKHORST
(Pires) 56
9. Francis JEFFERS

MATCH REPORT

Arsenal survived a courageous late comeback from Chelsea to claim a victory which saw them retain their five-point lead at the top of the Premiership. The Blues, meanwhile, lost their grip on second place to Manchester United who moved up the table courtesy of a late winner against Sunderland.

The Gunners had led for most of the match through a Desailly own goal, and had appeared to make the points safe through late efforts from van Bronckhorst and Henry.

But then Chelsea struck twice in two minutes and went agonisingly close to a stunning equaliser when a Gronkjaer cross narrowly eluded a gaggle of Chelsea players in the box.

In fact, the Blues had started brightly and De Lucas had squandered an early opening, slicing wide from the edge of the box, prior to the hosts taking the lead. Bergkamp slipped a neat pass to Pires, the Frenchman switched left to Cole, who delivered a teasing cross which narrowly eluded the charging Dutchman but was turned into his own net by Desailly.

Le Saux forced a sharp save from Seaman with a low 25-yarder, but then the Gunners seized the upper hand. Wiltord had one shot blocked by Melchiot and shaved an upright with another, then Vieira surged through the middle only for his final pass to be intercepted.

Cudicini's acrobatics prove in vain as Desailly's own goal opens the scoring.

2 CHELSEA

Stanic 85, Petit 86

23	Carlo CUDICINI
15	Mario MELCHIOT
13	William GALLAS
6	Marcel DESAILLY
3	Celestine BABAYARO
21	Enrique DE LUCAS
8	Frank LAMPARD
17	Emmanuel PETIT
14	Graeme LE SAUX
25	Gianfranco ZOLA
9	Jimmy Floyd HASSELBAINK

Arsenal remained in the ascendant after the break, with Bergkamp and Henry opening the Chelsea rearguard only for Gilberto to miscue, and Cudicini parrying a rasping drive from Henry. Their seemingly inevitable second goal materialised when van Bronckhorst won a crunching tackle and took a return pass from Henry before netting with a fearsome low cross-shot from 20 yards.

Within a minute Cudicini fumbled a routine Henry shot and it might have been all over, but Stanic nodded home from close range, then Seaman, under challenge from Hasselbaink, failed to gather a Gudjohnsen nod-on and Petit turned into an empty net.

All that remained was that late near-miss before the final whistle brought blessed relief.

Substitutes

1	Ed DE GOEY
26	John TERRY
12	Mario STANIC (Zola) 79
30	Jesper GRONKJAER (De Lucas) 56
22	Eidur GUDJOHNSEN (Le Saux) 70

Ashley Cole brushes aside the challenge of Enrique De Lucas.

A thunderous 20-yard drive from van Bronckhorst puts Arsenal 2-0 up.

FA Cup 3rd Round
Saturday 4 January 2003 at Highbury, 3 p.m.

ARSENAL 2

Bergkamp 15, McNiven og 67

1 David SEAMAN
22 Oleg LUZHNY
5 Martin KEOWN
20 Matthew UPSON
31 Giovanni VAN BRONCKHORST
28 Kolo TOURE
17 EDU
31 Sebastian SVARD
7 Robert PIRES
10 Dennis BERGKAMP
9 Francis JEFFERS

Substitutes

13 Stuart TAYLOR
26 Igors STEPANOVS
19 GILBERTO Silva (Svard) 77
35 David BENTLEY (Toure) 77
11 Sylvain WILTORD (Bergkamp) 80

MATCH REPORT

Dennis Bergkamp notched his century of goals for the Gunners as Arsène Wenger's side saw off the challenge of Third Division Oxford with a minimum of fuss.

Coming off an unbeaten run of eight matches and buoyed by the vociferous backing of 6,000 travelling fans, the visitors started so purposefully that Basham had the ball in Arsenal's net after only 58 seconds.

However, he was ruled marginally offside, and Oxford never mounted another notable threat. Instead the hosts, who had rested half-a-dozen regulars, assumed total control from the early moment when the Dutchman reached his landmark with a typically adroit clip from eight yards after good work by Jeffers.

After that Bergkamp ran the show, his delicate control and assured distribution a joy to behold, though Arsenal failed to

England under-19 skipper David Bentley came off the bench with the score at 2-0.

Dennis Bergkamp is first to Francis Jeffers' lay-off, clipping his shot over the advancing Woodman.

0 OXFORD UNITED

1	Andy WOODMAN
2	Scott McNIVEN
11	Matthew ROBINSON
5	Andy CROSBY
6	David WATERMAN
18	Matthew BOUND
4	David SAVAGE
21	Bob FORD
27	Roy HUNTER
22	David OLDFIELD
23	Steve BASHAM

Substitutes

28	Abdu SALL
12	Dean WHITEHEAD
10	Andrew SCOTT (Savage) 64
17	Jefferson LOUIS (Oldfield) 54
9	Lee STEELE (Basham) 84

capitalise on their first-half command, with Jeffers twice failing to register when sent through on goalkeeper Woodman.

The second half brought no change in the pattern, with the Gunners creating plenty of promising situations but without converting. Still, a giant-killing act was always possible while the margin remained at one, which it did until the three-quarter mark, when a Pires corner from the left was touched on at the near post and rebounded off the unfortunate McNiven into his own net from three yards.

Edu, Pires and Wiltord all might have added further goals, while the only tangible response from Oxford arrived after 70 minutes, courtesy of a forceful run by the energetic Louis, but that came to nothing when his fellow substitute Scott headed straight at Seaman from a promising position in front of goal.

As well as their place in the fourth round of the FA Cup, Arsenal could be delighted with the efforts of two youngsters. Svard turned in a neatly efficient performance in midfield, and the England under-19 skipper Bentley showed glimpses of skill and awareness during a late cameo appearance as a substitute for Toure.

BOOKINGS

Oxford United Ford 51, Robinson 60, Waterman 78

Top *Bergkamp celebrates the goal that his immaculate first-half performance merited.*
Bottom *Denmark under-21 international Sebastian Svard enjoys a rare first-team appearance against Oxford.*

FA Barclaycard Premiership
Sunday 12 January 2003 at St Andrew's, 4.30 p.m.

BIRMINGHAM CITY 0

18	Nico VAESEN
33	Ferdinand COLY
4	Steve VICKERS
17	Michael JOHNSON
2	Jeff KENNA
22	Damien JOHNSON
8	Robbie SAVAGE
32	Stephen CLEMENCE
23	Jamie CLAPHAM
21	Christophe DUGARRY
14	Stern JOHN

Substitutes

1	Ian BENNETT
3	Martin GRAINGER (Coly) 68
7	Paul DEVLIN (Clemence) 68
15	Jovan KIROVSKI (Dugarry) 86
27	Jonathan HUTCHINSON

Below *Thierry Henry races clear of the Birmingham defence.*
Right *Henry shows his gratitude to creator supreme Dennis Bergkamp.*

MATCH REPORT

A typically dashing display by Thierry Henry, whose brace of nerveless strikes completed his century of goals as a Gunner, was at the heart of this ruthlessly efficient demolition of toiling Birmingham City.

Handing Premiership baptisms to four new recruits, including French World Cup winner Christophe Dugarry, the Blues lacked coherence in the face of Arsenal's slickly orchestrated approach play and deadly finishing.

Wiltord fired an early warning but his volley skewed wide, and although Dugarry responded with a fierce left-footer which whistled past an upright, soon the hosts' brittle defence was breached with devastating simplicity.

Bergkamp took possession in midfield while Henry outpaced the Birmingham rearguard before accepting the Dutchman's precise dispatch, swerving past Vaesen and depositing the ball firmly into the waiting net.

The Gunners continued to dominate and Edu's far-post volley demanded a superb save from Vaesen, then Henry drove into the side-netting after inventive work by Bergkamp and Pires.

Midway through the first half Birmingham rallied, and a Clapham 25-yarder had Seaman plunging to parry, but the Champions' reaction was devastating, Pires capitalising on hesitation by Michael Johnson to lash home from 20 yards.

The Blues fought on, with Dugarry their main danger, but when he skipped past Campbell his shot was high, then Seaman smothered a header from John.

4 ARSENAL

Henry 6, 70, Pires 29, Lauren 67

1. David SEAMAN
12. LAUREN
5. Martin KEOWN
23. Sol CAMPBELL
3. Ashley COLE
11. Sylvain WILTORD
19. GILBERTO Silva
17. EDU
7. Robert PIRES
10. Dennis BERGKAMP
14. Thierry HENRY

Substitutes

13. Stuart TAYLOR
22. Oleg LUZHNY
16. Giovanni VAN BRONCKHORST (Edu) 76
28. Kolo TOURE (Pires) 80
9. Francis JEFFERS (Bergkamp) 78

They maintained their momentum briefly after the break, but two Arsenal strikes in the space of three minutes put paid to their comeback hopes. First Bergkamp clipped a cross from the left and Lauren's header was deflected in via the shoulder of the unlucky Michael Johnson, then Pires linked sweetly with Wiltord, whose neat lay-off enabled Henry to rack up his hundred by steering past Vaesen.

The Frenchman almost commenced his second century with a 25-yard curler which flashed inches wide. By then Birmingham must have been wishing the floodlight failure which delayed kick-off had been of rather longer duration.

BOOKINGS

Birmingham City Coly 21, D Johnson 90

Arsenal Lauren 32, Keown 59

Robert Pires crashes home Arsenal's second goal as a helpless Steve Vickers looks on.

FA Barclaycard Premiership
Sunday 19 January 2003 at Highbury, 2 p.m.

ARSENAL   3

Henry 14 pen, 71, 87

1   David SEAMAN
12   LAUREN
5   Martin KEOWN
23   Sol CAMPBELL
16   Giovanni VAN BRONCKHORST
11   Sylvain WILTORD
19   GILBERTO Silva
17   EDU
7   Robert PIRES
10   Dennis BERGKAMP
14   Thierry HENRY

Substitutes

13   Stuart TAYLOR
22   Oleg LUZHNY (Wiltord) 87
28   Kolo TOURE
15   Ray PARLOUR (Edu) 68
9   Francis JEFFERS (Bergkamp) 87

MATCH REPORT

A Thierry Henry hat-trick, including a rare header, wrapped up a controversial but ultimately comprehensive victory over luckless West Ham.

Arsenal's French marksman was at his irresistible best, but the match hinged on two contentious moments and the referee ruled in the Gunners' favour both times.

First he red-carded Lomas for his penalty-box challenge on Pires, who had been sent in by Bergkamp, and Henry opened the scoring from the spot.

Then, after the ten-man Hammers had equalised, Bergkamp appeared to catch Bowyer in the face before delivering a cross which Henry nodded home at the far post. The goal was allowed to stand and thereafter the Champions tightened their grip on the game.

West Ham had begun brightly, though Arsenal might have snatched the lead when a pinpoint Pires delivery narrowly eluded Bergkamp, who was untended three yards out.

Robert Pires is impeded by West Ham's Steve Lomas, who concedes a 14th-minute penalty.

Soon the penalty incident established the hosts' ascendancy, and the visitors might have been sunk without trace but for an exceptional display by James. Three times in 15 minutes he pulled off brilliant saves, two of them at point-blank range, to frustrate the rampant Henry and he plunged headlong to tip away a cleverly disguised 16-yarder from Bergkamp.

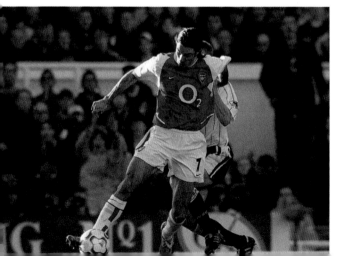

1 WEST HAM UNITED

Defoe 40

1	David JAMES
7	Christian DAILLY
19	Ian PEARCE
15	Gary BREEN
3	Nigel WINTERBURN
11	Steve LOMAS
5	Lee BOWYER
25	Edouard CISSE
8	Trevor SINCLAIR
26	Joe COLE
9	Jermain DEFOE

Substitutes

17	Raimond VAN DER GOUW
23	Glen JOHNSON
20	Scott MINTO (Winterburn) 82
16	John MONCUR (Cisse) 85
4	Don HUTCHISON

Yet suddenly West Ham relieved the siege when Edu's sloppy back-pass was intercepted by Defoe, who swept his shot past Seaman from 12 yards.

The second half produced almost constant Arsenal pressure, with Wiltord, van Bronckhorst and Keown all going close to restoring home advantage, but Glenn Roeder's men clung on valiantly until that decisive second strike.

Finally, the Gunners fashioned a goal about which there could not be the slightest reservation when Parlour took possession on the right, then switched inside to Pires, whose raking crossfield dispatch reached Henry in full stride. The finish, from eight yards, was perfect.

BOOKINGS

Arsenal Bergkamp 50, Lauren 83, Parlour 85
West Ham United Breen 10

DISMISSALS

West Ham United Lomas 13

Top, left *Former Gunner Nigel Winterburn attempts to halt the progress of Ray Parlour.*

Top, Right *Thierry Henry manages to steer his shot around the considerable frame of David James to complete his hat-trick.*

77

FA Cup 4th Round
Saturday 25 January 2003 at Highbury, 3 p.m.

FARNBOROUGH TOWN   1

Baptiste 71

1	Tony PENNOCK
10	Christian LEE
24	Darren ANNON
5	Nathan BUNCE
3	Justin GREGORY
16	Danny CARROLL
20	Gary HOLLOWAY
7	Steve WATSON
2	Michael WARNER
22	Rocky BAPTISTE
18	Ken CHARLERY

Substitutes

11	Tony TAGGART
19	Gary BUTTERWORTH (Charlery) 80
8	Lenny PIPER (Carroll) 86
14	Chris PIPER (Holloway) 76
9	Joff VANSITTART

Sol Campbell climbs highest to head home the opening goal.

MATCH REPORT

For once Arsenal were the visitors at Highbury, Farnborough having elected to switch the tie from Cherrywood Road to the FA Cup holders' own turf, but there was never any question about who looked more at home.

The Conference side battled gamely enough, but after conceding two goals in four minutes midway through the first half and then being reduced to ten men by the sending-off of Lee, the outcome was inevitable.

Though the two clubs were separated by 102 places in the League pyramid, Farnborough held their own until Campbell opened the scoring with a thumping header from van Bronckhorst's corner. They were still reeling from that blow when Lauren and Pires sent Toure to the byline, and Jeffers converted clinically at the near post.

Now the Gunners were dominant and, after Pennock had made a full-length save to divert a Pires volley, Town were reduced to

5 ARSENAL

Campbell 19, Jeffers 23, 68, Bergkamp 74, Lauren 79

13	Stuart TAYLOR
12	LAUREN
23	Sol CAMPBELL
18	Pascal CYGAN
16	Giovanni VAN BRONCKHORST
7	Robert PIRES
15	Ray PARLOUR
4	Patrick VIEIRA
28	Kolo TOURE
25	Nwankwo KANU
9	Francis JEFFERS

Substitutes

1	David SEAMAN
22	Oleg LUZHNY
17	EDU (Kanu) 76
10	Dennis BERGKAMP (Pires) 66
11	Sylvain WILTORD (Toure) 66

ten men when Lee was dismissed for pulling back Jeffers as the striker was racing on to a Parlour through-ball.

Farnborough stuck to their task, though, and early in the second half Watson hit a stinging 20-yard drive which Taylor parried for a corner. Arsenal's response was devastating, van Bronckhorst crossing for Jeffers to celebrate his 22nd birthday with his second goal, a simple header from four yards.

Back came the underdogs, and this time their efforts bore fruit as Baptiste slipped past Cygan, Taylor managing to block the big centre-forward's first shot, only to be beaten by his second.

Farnborough's fans raised a smile with their rendition of 'You're not singing any more', but the Gunners were not slow to retort. First Cygan made amends for his earlier mistake with a lovely pass to van Bronckhorst, whose centre was tapped in by Bergkamp, then Lauren ran on to a Bergkamp chip, rounded a challenge and netted neatly.

More goals might have followed, but that would have been unduly harsh on the gallant, er, hosts.

BOOKINGS
Farnborough Town Carroll 8,
Charlery 74

DISMISSALS
Farnborough Town Lee 28

Top, left *Francis Jeffers converts Toure's cross with an accurate header.* **Left** *Lauren completes the scoring with a clinical finish past the advancing Tony Pennock.*

FA Barclaycard Premiership
Wednesday 29 January 2003 at Anfield, 8 p.m.

LIVERPOOL 2

Riise 52, Heskey 90

1	Jerzy DUDEK
23	Jamie CARRAGHER
2	Stephane HENCHOZ
4	Sami HYYPIA
18	John Arne RIISE
9	El Hadji DIOUF
17	Steven GERRARD
13	Danny MURPHY
28	Bruno CHEYROU
8	Emile HESKEY
10	Michael OWEN

Substitutes

19	Pegguy ARPHEXAD
30	Djimi TRAORE
21	Salif DIAO (Murphy) 80
7	Vladimir SMICER (Cheyrou) 69
5	Milan BAROS (Diouf) 82

Bottom, left *Robert Pires slides home the opening goal.*
Bottom, right *Thierry Henry gets the better of Liverpool's Stephane Henchoz.*

MATCH REPORT

Arsenal outplayed battling Liverpool comprehensively throughout most of an entertaining contest, only for victory to be snatched from their grasp by a controversial stoppage-time strike.

The Gunners bestrode Anfield with their consummate class and created an avalanche of scoring opportunities, some arising out of slick team play, many more the product of Thierry Henry's blistering pace and delicious flair.

Yet it was the hosts who made the more forceful start, with Heskey evading Cygan and Cole before crossing to Owen, who failed to make clean contact from ten yards.

Arsenal's riposte was deadly. Bergkamp found space on the right and speared a typically probing delivery into the path of Henry, whose shot was blocked by Dudek. Unfortunately for Liverpool, the ball ricocheted to Pires, who sidefooted into the vacant net from 12 yards.

Now the Gunners took command. Henry mesmerised three defenders only for Dudek to block his shot, then Vieira netted with a header only for the 'goal' to be ruled out for pushing.

Seaman's trailing leg prevented a breakaway equaliser from Owen, but soon the visitors fashioned five clear chances in the

2 ARSENAL

Pires 8, Bergkamp 63

1	David SEAMAN
12	LAUREN
23	Sol CAMPBELL
18	Pascal CYGAN
3	Ashley COLE
15	Ray PARLOUR
19	GILBERTO Silva
4	Patrick VIERA
7	Robert PIRES
10	Dennis BERGKAMP
14	Thierry HENRY

space of seven rampant minutes. However, Henry (twice) and Vieira were denied by Dudek, Cheyrou cleared a Cygan header off the line and Bergkamp untypically miscontrolled a centre from Henry.

Owen and Heskey both missed openings as Liverpool revived shortly before the break, but Henry might have bagged a brace early in the second period as the first-half pattern re-emerged.

Briefly the Gunners were rocked by a Riise 20-yarder which gave Seaman no chance, but the lead was regained when Bergkamp's speculative shot from the edge of the box was deflected past the overworked Dudek by Henchoz.

Thereafter Arsenal were cruising, with Dudek making more fine saves from Henry and Gilberto, but in the 91st minute the referee awarded Liverpool a hotly disputed corner. The ball reached Diao, whose precise cross was nodded in by the persistent Heskey, and somehow two points had slipped away.

Substitutes

13	Stuart TAYLOR
22	Oleg LUZHNY (Bergkamp) 86
16	Giovanni VAN BRONCKHORST
11	Sylvain WILTORD
9	Francis JEFFERS

BOOKINGS

Liverpool Diouf 65

Arsenal Cygan 42

FA Barclaycard Premiership	29 January 2002						
	P	W	D	L	F	A	Pts
ARSENAL	25	16	5	4	54	27	53
Newcastle United	25	15	3	7	41	31	48
Manchester United	24	14	5	5	40	24	47
Chelsea	25	12	8	5	44	25	44
Everton	25	12	6	7	32	30	42
Liverpool	25	10	9	6	34	25	39
Southampton	25	10	9	6	28	23	39
Tottenham Hotspur	25	11	5	9	35	35	38
Manchester City	25	11	4	10	36	35	37
Charlton Athletic	25	10	6	9	31	32	36
Blackburn Rovers	25	8	10	7	31	28	34
Aston Villa	25	9	5	11	27	27	32
Leeds United	25	9	4	12	33	32	31
Middlesbrough	25	8	6	11	29	29	30
Fulham	24	7	6	11	25	31	27
Birmingham City	24	6	8	10	20	32	26
Bolton Wanderers	25	4	9	12	25	41	21
West Ham United	25	4	8	13	28	48	20
Sunderland	25	4	7	14	16	35	19
West Bromwich Albion	24	4	5	15	17	36	17

Dennis Bergkamp fires in a shot that is deflected past Jerzy Dudek.

FA Barclaycard Premiership
Saturday 1 February 2003 at Highbury, 3 p.m.

ARSENAL 2
Pires 17, 90

1 David SEAMAN
12 LAUREN
5 Martin KEOWN
23 Sol CAMPBELL
3 Ashley COLE
11 Sylvain WILTORD
19 GILBERTO Silva
4 Patrick VIEIRA
7 Robert PIRES
10 Dennis BERGKAMP
14 Thierry HENRY

Substitutes

13 Stuart TAYLOR
18 Pascal CYGAN
28 Kolo TOURE (Lauren) 84
16 Giovanni VAN BRONCKHORST
(Gilberto) 79
9 Francis JEFFERS (Wiltord) 70)

MATCH REPORT

Highbury erupted in a collective roar of exultation and relief as a stoppage-time winner from Robert Pires denied Fulham their first point on Arsenal turf since 1964.

In terms of possession and scoring opportunities, the Gunners deserved their victory, but only just. Jean Tigana's team had forced them to fight all the way, which had not seemed likely as the Champions got off to a jet-propelled start.

The game was not half a minute old when Wiltord broke down the right and passed inside to Henry, who swivelled neatly past a near-post challenge only to be crowded out in the act of shooting.

Fulham countered gamely, with Boa Morte almost setting up Sava, only for Arsenal to take the lead with a beautifully worked goal. Vieira seized possession in midfield and pushed the ball forward to Bergkamp, whose first-time pass located Henry on the left; the Frenchman bobbed and weaved before floating a perfect cross to Pires, who headed home unopposed at the far post.

Now the Highbury faithful sat back in anticipation of a rout, but the visitors were having none of it, and they equalised when Finnan's deep cross from the right was nodded back by Marlet for Malbranque to volley a low shot into the far corner of Seaman's net from 15 yards.

The Gunners almost regained the upper hand shortly before the break when a dazzling dash by Henry took him past Finnan and Melville, but he was foiled by Taylor at the angle of the six-yard box.

Francis Jeffers puts the Fulham defence on the back foot.

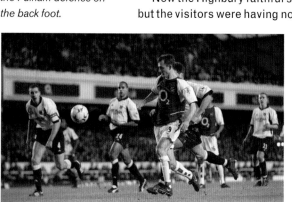

82

1 FULHAM

Malbranque 29

1	Maik TAYLOR
2	Steve FINNAN
17	Martin DJETOU
24	Alain GOMA
26	Jon HARLEY
23	Sean DAVIS
18	Sylvain LEGWINSKI
14	Steed MALBRANQUE
11	Luis BOA MORTE
7	Steve MARLET
9	Facundo SAVA

Substitutes

21	Martin HERRERA
4	Andy MELVILLE (Legwinski) 10
27	Pierre WOME
19	Bjarne GOLDBAEK
20	Louis SAHA (Sava) 69

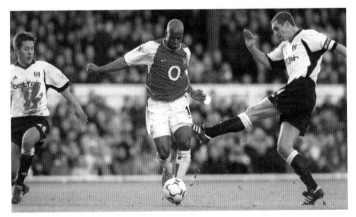

BOOKINGS

Arsenal Lauren 10, Henry 69,
Toure 87

Fulham Melville 89

As the second period progressed, the hosts' pressure mounted, but so did their fans' apprehension as Taylor saved smartly from a Bergkamp header, then fisted away a savage volley from substitute Jeffers.

When the lively striker's lay-off was driven against an upright by Gilberto, it seemed that anti-climax was inevitable, but then Vieira, van Bronckhorst and Jeffers combined sweetly to send in Pires for a tap-in that saved the day.

Top *Robert Pires heads home the opening goal at the far post.*

Bottom *Fulham's Andy Melville takes a wild swing as Wiltord advances.*

NEWCASTLE UNITED 1

Robert 53

1 Shay GIVEN
18 Aaron HUGHES
5 Andy O'BRIEN
19 Titus BRAMBLE
35 Olivier BERNARD
4 Nolberto SOLANO
7 Jemaine JENAS
8 Kieron DYER
32 Laurent ROBERT
10 Craig BELLAMY
9 Alan SHEARER

Substitutes

24 Tony CAIG
34 Nikos DABIZAS
11 Gary SPEED (Solano) 46
20 Lomano LUA LUA
23 Shola AMEOBI (Shearer) 90

MATCH REPORT

Arsenal ended Newcastle's run of 11 straight Premiership victories on Tyneside, but failed to take advantage of the Magpies being reduced to ten men for the final third of a frenetic encounter by the dismissal of Laurent Robert.

The Gunners were in command for long periods, creating more scoring opportunities than their hosts, and were disappointed not to stretch their lead at the top of the table to five points.

The match began at a cracking pace and both sides went close to snatching an early lead. First Robert hared down the left before delivering a tantalising low cross which Shearer nudged goalwards, forcing Seaman to make a scrambling save at the foot of the far post.

Arsenal retaliated briskly and the Magpies had a double escape after 12 minutes when Henry's corner was met by a thunderous close-range header by

ilberto resists the challenge of Newcastle's ermaine Jenas to retain possession.

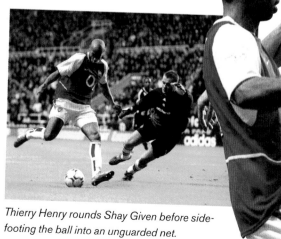

Thierry Henry rounds Shay Given before side-footing the ball into an unguarded net.

1 ARSENAL

Henry 35

1 David SEAMAN
12 LAUREN
5 Martin KEOWN
23 Sol CAMPBELL
3 Ashley COLE
11 Sylvain WILTORD
19 GILBERTO Silva
4 Patrick VIEIRA
7 Robert PIRES
10 Dennis BERGKAMP
14 Thierry HENRY

Substitutes

13 Stuart TAYLOR
18 Pascal CYGAN
16 Giovanni VAN BRONKHORST
(Wiltord) 85
15 Ray PARLOUR (Gilberto) 85
9 Francis JEFFERS (Bergkamp) 78

Vieira, Solano's goal-line clearance bounced off the underside of the bar and Pires nodded the rebound high from one yard.

Next Shearer's superb 15-yard volley from Solano's cross was caught by Seaman, but then the Gunners seized the initiative and were denied in astonishing fashion when Henry's cross was deflected by Bramble, only for Given to clear with a flying header.

Three minutes later, though, the visitors went ahead when Henry raced on to a delightful flick from Wiltord, rounded the goalkeeper and sidefooted into the empty net.

Given saved smartly from both Wiltord and Pires, but Robert transformed the atmosphere with a piece of brilliance, darting between Lauren and Vieira and beating Seaman with a low 20-yarder. Soon, though, he was sent off for a second bookable offence. Now Arsenal poured forward but Newcastle resisted nobly, O'Brien blocking a Bergkamp drive and Given frustrating Vieira. Finally Bellamy almost brought the house down in stoppage time when his deflected cross appeared goalbound, but the back-pedalling Seaman saved the day.

BOOKINGS

Newcastle United Shearer 29, Robert 56
Arsenal Lauren 22, Cole 87

DISMISSALS

Newcastle United Robert 58

Three musketeers: the all-French trio of Henry, Pires and Wiltord celebrate the game's opening goal.

85

FA Cup 5th Round
Saturday 15 February 2003 at Old Trafford, 12.15 p.m.

MANCHESTER UNITED 0

1 Fabien BARTHEZ
2 Gary NEVILLE
6 Rio FERDINAND
24 Wesley BROWN
27 Mikael SILVESTRE
7 David BECKHAM
16 Roy KEANE
18 Paul SCHOLES
20 Ole Gunnar SOLSKJAER
11 Ryan GIGGS
10 Ruud VAN NISTELROOY

Substitutes

19 RICARDO
3 Phil NEVILLE
22 John O'SHEA
8 Nicky BUTT (Beckham) 83
21 Diego FORLAN (Giggs) 71

Edu curls a free-kick which deflects off Beckham's shoulder to beat Barthez.

MATCH REPORT

Arsenal passed their way to an emphatic victory over their chief domestic rivals, although United were kicking themselves for missing a succession of golden scoring opportunities.

After a tumultuous start in which Scholes, van Nistelrooy and Vieira were yellow-carded, the action seesawed from end to end, with the hosts creating the clearest early opening when Giggs set up Solskjaer, whose shot against Seaman's near post cannoned to safety.

The Gunners forced a succession of corners, and Barthez was forced to save with his feet when Wiltord fired through a forest of legs. Back came United, but Solskjaer sliced wildly from a mis-cued Campbell clearance and Keown halted a van Nistelrooy surge before Giggs was guilty of an astonishing miss.

Racing on to a through-ball from Beckham, the Welshman nipped past Seaman and evaded Campbell to be faced with an empty net. A simple side-foot would have sufficed but somehow he clipped his 18-yard shot over the bar with his unfavoured right foot.

Arsenal's response was deadly if decidely fortunate, Edu's 22-yard free-kick rebounding from Beckham's shoulder and into the far corner of the net with Barthez hopelessly wrong-footed.

Now the Gunners took an iron grip on proceedings, with Pires, Edu and

2 ARSENAL

Edu 35, Wiltord 52

1	David SEAMAN
12	LAUREN
5	Martin KEOWN
23	Sol CAMPBELL
3	Ashley COLE
15	Ray PARLOUR
4	Patrick VIEIRA
17	EDU
7	Robert PIRES
11	Sylvain WILTORD
9	Francis JEFFERS

Substitutes

20	Guillaume WARMUZ
18	Pascal CYGAN
16	Giovanni VAN BRONCKHORST
	(Pires) 84
28	Kolo TOURE (Wiltord) 90
14	Thierry HENRY (Jeffers) 73

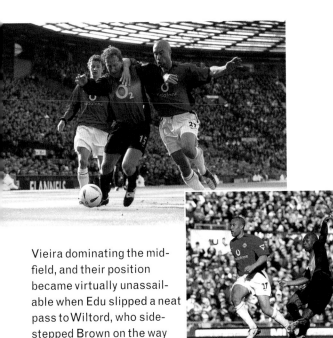

Vieira dominating the midfield, and their position became virtually unassailable when Edu slipped a neat pass to Wiltord, who sidestepped Brown on the way to netting clinically from 15 yards.

BOOKINGS

Manchester United Scholes 3, van Nistelrooy 4, Keane 29

Arsenal Vieira 7

United hit back, and although their attacks were more frenzied than measured, they did fashion two wonderful chances to reduce the arrears. First Beckham's floater found Giggs untended only six yards from goal, but he mis-volleyed, then the similarly unmarked Solskjaer headed a Keane delivery into Seaman's side netting from even closer range.

After that the hosts barely threatened, and Arsenal went close to another goal when Wiltord latched on to a beautiful through-ball from Henry, but was foiled by Brown's last-ditch challenge.

Above, left *Ray Parlour goes shoulder to shoulder with United's Mikael Silvestre.*
Above, right *Sylvain Wiltord scores at Old Trafford for the second season in a row.*

ARSENAL 1

Wiltord 5

1 David SEAMAN

12 LAUREN

23 Sol CAMPBELL

18 Pascal CYGAN

3 Ashley COLE

11 Sylvain WILTORD

4 Patrick VIEIRA

19 GILBERTO Silva

7 Robert PIRES

10 Dennis BERGKAMP

14 Thierry HENRY

Substitutes

13 Stuart TAYLOR (Seaman) 46

26 Igors STEPANOVS

16 Giovanni VAN BRONCKHORST

15 Ray PARLOUR

17 EDU

25 Nwankwo KANU (Bergkamp) 84

9 Francis JEFFERS (Gilberto) 72

MATCH REPORT

Arsenal began with a flourish and appeared to assume command, but it proved to be an illusion as the Dutch domestic double-winners surged back into contention and went perilously close to snatching a late victory.

Vieira had already headed wide during the Gunners' fast start when Bergkamp found Wiltord free on the right and the Frenchman cut inside and opened the scoring with a near-post drive.

At this point Ajax seemed nonplussed by their hosts' pace, purpose and invention and soon afterwards Henry jinked smoothly past two challenges before firing narrowly wide.

But suddenly the atmosphere was transformed when Galasek lofted a pass from the centre circle and De Jong stole behind Cole to clip a crisp cross-shot beyond Seaman from eight yards.

A minute later it took a thunderous challenge from Campbell to thwart Ibrahimovic in the act of shooting, and thereafter the visitors grew in confidence, their passing assured and inventive, their defence formidably tight.

The remainder of the first half was attractive and evenly contested. Lobont saved two Henry snap-shots and Pires was twice off-target, while Seaman dealt with efforts from Chivu and Maxwell, and raced from his line to foil van der Meyde.

After the break the Gunners exerted

Dennis Bergkamp nonchalantly flicks the ball over the head of an Ajax defender.

1 AJAX

De Jong 17

some pressure and Gilberto might have restored the lead after 53 minutes, but shot tamely and Lobont saved. The closest Arsenal came to a breakthrough was through Bergkamp's sudden, clever

1	Bogdan LOBONT
2	Hatem TRABELSI
16	Petri PASENEN
5	Christian CHIVU
24	Jelle VAN DAMME
26	Nigel DE JONG
4	Tomas GALASEK
13	Scherer MAXWELL
10	Steven PIENAAR
7	Andy VAN DER MEYDE
9	Zlatan IBRAHIMOVIC
Substitutes	
21	Joey DIDULICA
3	Andre BERGDOLMO
15	Wesley SNEIJDER
8	Richard WITSCHGE (van Damme) 76
22	Abubakari YAKUBU (Pienaar) 90
28	Nourdin BOUKHARI (Ibrahimovic)
30	Stefano SEEDORF

BOOKINGS

Arsenal Pires 90
Ajax Pasenen 56, Lobont 77, Boukhari 81

20-yarder after 71 minutes, but the ball skidded to safety off the outside of a post.

Meanwhile Ibrahimovic had missed from a De Jong free-kick and, five minutes from time, a van der Meyde cross was turned wide from close range by Boukhari with Taylor at full stretch. The last chance of the match fell to Kanu, but he volleyed high from Jeffers' flick.

Above, left *Sol Campbell holds off Ajax's Steven Pienaar and surges forward from defence.*
Left *Thierry Henry congratulates his goalscoring compatriot Sylvain Wiltord.*

FA Barclaycard Premiership
Saturday 22 February 2003 at Maine Road, 3 p.m.

MANCHESTER CITY 1

Anelka 87

20	Carlo NASH
22	Richard DUNNE
24	Steve HOWEY
17	Sun JIHAI
2	David SOMMEIL
31	Djamel BELMADI
14	Eyal BERKOVIC
23	Marc-Vivien FOE
3	Niclas JENSEN
33	Robbie FOWLER
39	Nicolas ANELKA

Substitutes

12	Nicky WEAVER
6	Kevin HORLOCK
8	Ali BENARBIA (Belmadi) 65
29	Shaun WRIGHT-PHILLIPS
	(Dunne) 46
10	Shaun GOATER

Below, left *Goalscorer Dennis Bergkamp is engulfed in a huddle of team-mates.*

Below, right *Sol Campbell makes it 4-0 with this 19th-minute header.*

MATCH REPORT

Arsenal destroyed Manchester City with a devastating four-goal blitz in the opening 19 minutes of their final visit to Maine Road, stretching their lead at the Premiership summit to five points in the process.

Bizarrely in the light of the imminent rout, it was City who threatened first when Sommeil sent Fowler scampering clear on the left, but his cross was too far ahead of Anelka.

The Gunners' response was utterly crushing. First Vieira, Wiltord and Lauren worked the ball to Bergkamp, who was mysteriously unattended in front of goal and he made no mistake from eight yards.

Next Dunne, who had been culpable for the Dutchman's breakthrough, mishit a clearance which was pounced upon by Henry; he danced along the left byline and pulled back for Pires to sweep home on 12 minutes.

The third goal was both simple and sublime. Keown dispatched a raking free-kick which Henry controlled on his right instep as it dropped over his shoulder, then arrowed an instant left-foot volley across Nash and inside the far post from 20 yards.

5 ARSENAL

Bergkamp 4, Pires 12, Henry 15, Campbell 19, Vieira 53

13	Stuart TAYLOR
12	LAUREN
23	Sol CAMPBELL
5	Martin KEOWN
16	Giovanni VAN BRONCKHORST
11	Sylvain WILTORD
19	GILBERTO Silva
4	Patrick VIEIRA
7	Robert PIRES
10	Dennis BERGKAMP
14	Thierry HENRY

Substitutes

20	Guillaume WARMUZ
18	Pascal CYGAN
17	EDU (Pires) 74
15	Ray PARLOUR (Bergkamp) 64
9	Francis JEFFERS (Wiltord) 74

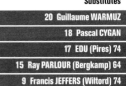

City were still reeling when the untameable Henry earned a corner, which he directed unerringly on to the head of Campbell, and that was 4-0.

BOOKINGS

Arsenal Cole 40, Vieira 75

Shortly before the interval Kevin Keegan's men might have pulled one back but Taylor blocked a Fowler volley from Belmadi's cross. However, that represented only a lull in the one-way traffic, which resumed in the second half with a sweeping Arsenal move, halted only when Nash saved from Henry with an outstretched foot. The beleaguered goalkeeper was helpless, though, when faced with Vieira, who slotted in the fifth after swapping passes with Bergkamp.

Now, understandably, the Gunners eased off a little, which enabled Taylor, standing in for the injured Seaman, to demonstrate his prowess. Accordingly he made five outstanding stops, diving athletically to frustrate Anelka, Fowler twice, Wright-Phillips and Berkovic before being beaten at close range by Anelka near the death.

Above, left *Thierry Henry fires home a dipping volley for Arsenal's third goal.*
Above, right *Stuart Taylor enjoyed an impressive return to first-team duty at Maine Road.*

AJAX   0

1	Bogdan LOBONT
2	Hatem TREBELSI
16	Petri PASANEN
5	Christian CHIVU
8	Richard WITSCHGE
10	Steven PIENAAR
4	Tomas GALASEK
13	Scherer MAXWELL
26	Nigel DE JONG
7	Andy VAN DER MEYDE
9	Zlatan IBRAHIMOVIC

Substitutes

21	Joey DIDULICA
3	Andre BERGDOLMO
15	Wesley SNEIJDER (Pienaar) 90
22	Abubakari YAKUBU (Galasek) 70
24	Jelle VAN DAMME
28	Nourdin BOUKHARI
11	Ahmed Hossam MIDO (Zlatan) 84

MATCH REPORT

Usually it is Arsenal's flair which rivets the eye, but when patience and resolution were demanded in a cagey tactical battle with the Dutch Champions, the Gunners were not found wanting.

However, although the goalless stalemate was enough to ensure the two protagonists shared leadership of their Champions League group, it left Arsène Wenger to contemplate a recent record of only one win in seven European outings.

Ajax began with a slick 50-second passing movement, but it was Arsenal who mounted the first goal threat when Henry sidestepped his marker and hit a fizzing drive from the right angle of the box, which demanded a plunging save from Lobont.

Long-range efforts from Gilberto and Wiltord did not trouble the 'keeper, and finally Ajax launched a telling attack when Trebelsi cut in from the right and found Ibrahimovic, whose shot was deflected wide by Keown.

Pires' delicious nutmegging of Galasek led to a tame cross-shot from Bergkamp, then Lobont blocked a close-range effort

Below *Dennis Bergkamp out-muscles an Ajax defender.*

A determined Bergkamp controls the ball on his thigh as he attempts to find a path to goal.

0 ARSENAL

from Vieira, but it was the Gunners who survived the closest shave of the first period when Cole headed off his line from a Chivu free-kick.

Shortly after the restart a brisk intervention from Lauren thwarted another combination between Trebelsi and Ibrahimovic, but with goalmouth incident on the sparse side, it was Arsenal who continued to show the most enterprise.

Lobont tipped over a trademark 30-yard Henry free-kick, then the 'keeper was perfectly positioned to take Vieira's firm half-volley from the angle of the six-yard box following a beautifully flighted cross from the right flank by Bergkamp.

Ajax continued to pass crisply but stationed so many men behind the ball that they offered little further menace, and the final thrust came from the visitors when Henry nodded on to van Bronckhorst, whose clever half-volleyed cross narrowly eluded the sprinting Jeffers.

| 1 David SEAMAN |
| 12 LAUREN |
| 23 Sol CAMPBELL |
| 5 Martin KEOWN |
| 3 Ashley COLE |
| 11 Sylvain WILTORD |
| 19 GILBERTO Silva |
| 4 Patrick VIEIRA |
| 7 Robert PIRES |
| 10 Dennis BERGKAMP |
| 14 Thierry HENRY |

Substitutes

| 13 Stuart TAYLOR |
| 18 Pascal CYGAN |
| 17 EDU |
| 15 Ray PARLOUR (Wiltord) 79 |
| 16 Giovanni VAN BRONCKHORST |
| (Pires) 86 |
| 28 Kolo TOURE |
| 9 Francis JEFFERS (Bergkamp) 79 |

BOOKINGS

Arsenal Cole 40, Vieira 75

FA Barclaycard Premiership	26 February 2003						
	P	W	D	L	F	A	Pts
ARSENAL	28	18	6	4	62	30	60
Manchester United	28	16	7	5	45	26	55
Newcastle United	27	16	4	7	45	32	52
Chelsea	28	13	9	6	49	29	48
Everton	28	14	6	8	37	33	48
Charlton Athletic	28	13	6	9	39	34	45
Liverpool	28	11	10	7	39	28	43
Tottenham Hotspur	28	12	7	9	41	38	43
Blackburn Rovers	28	10	10	8	34	32	40
Southampton	28	10	9	9	29	28	39
Manchester City	28	11	5	12	39	43	38
Aston Villa	28	10	5	13	31	32	35
Middlesbrough	27	9	7	11	33	31	34
Leeds United	28	10	4	14	34	37	34
Fulham	28	9	7	12	32	35	34
Birmingham City	28	7	8	13	25	41	29
Bolton Wanderers	28	5	11	12	31	45	26
West Ham United	28	5	8	15	30	53	23
West Bromwich Albion	28	5	6	17	21	43	21
Sunderland	28	4	7	17	19	45	19

ARSENAL 2

Jeffers 25, Pires 45

1 David SEAMAN

28 Kolo TOURE

23 Sol CAMPBELL

5 Martin KEOWN

16 Giovanni VAN BRONCKHORST

8 Fredrik LJUNGBERG

15 Ray PARLOUR

17 EDU

7 Robert PIRES

14 Thierry HENRY

9 Francis JEFFERS

Substitutes

20 Guillavme WARMUZ

18 Pascal CYGAN

21 Jermaine PENNANT

19 GILBERTO Silva (Pires) 69

11 Sylvain WILTORD (Ljungberg) 64

Francis Jeffers converts Thierry Henry's accurate pass to open the scoring.

MATCH REPORT

With Manchester United taking a break from Premiership action to contest the League Cup Final, Arsenal re-established an eight-point lead at the top of the Premiership with a deserved victory over Charlton.

The Addicks could have no complaints over the result, and the margin of Arsenal's victory might have been greater than the two goals created by the incandescent talent of Thierry Henry. The Frenchman ran at defenders to destructive effect, and the visitors had no answer to him.

As befits a top-six team that had suffered only one defeat in 15 League outings, the visitors opened purposefully and after ten minutes Seaman dived briskly to repel Euell's firm drive following a neat build-up from Parker and Powell.

But the Gunners wrested control and almost took the lead after 15 minutes when Fish misjudged a bounce and Henry's shot beat Kiely but rebounded from a post.

Next a Jeffers shot was blocked by Powell and Kiely parried brilliantly from Pires before the irresistible Henry engineered the breakthrough. Swivelling past a challenge on the left, he darted

0 CHARLTON ATHLETIC

1	Dean KIELY
19	Luke YOUNG
24	Jonathan FORTUNE
6	Mark FISH
3	Chris POWELL
2	Radostin KISHISHEV
9	Jason EUELL
7	Scott PARKER
10	Claus JENSEN
17	Shaun BARTLETT
23	Kevin LISBIE

Substitutes

22	Ben ROBERTS
18	Paul KONCHESKY (Powell) 79
30	Tahar EL KHALEJ
20	Mathias SVENSSON (Parker) 88
21	Jonatan JOHANSSON (Bartlett) 59

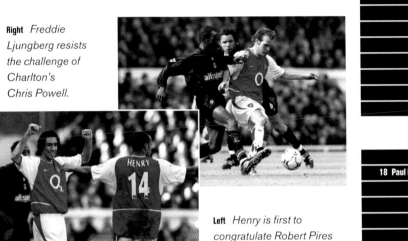

Right *Freddie Ljungberg resists the challenge of Charlton's Chris Powell.*

Left *Henry is first to congratulate Robert Pires on a rare headed goal.*

BOOKINGS

Arsenal Henry 31

into the box and stroked a diagonal pass with the outside of his right boot for Jeffers to supply a simple close-range finish.

A minute later Lisbie was only fractionally off target with a volley on the turn, but that was an isolated example of Charlton menace as Arsenal poured forward. Kiely could be proud of his plunge to hold a sudden 30-yarder from Parlour, but he was beaten again in first-half stoppage time when another left-wing surge from Henry resulted in a Powell miskick, Ljungberg nudged the rebound against a post and Pires nodded in the loose ball.

After the break Fish headed into Seaman's side-netting from a Jensen corner, but apart from that it was one-way traffic. Henry set up Pires but he sidefooted wide from ten yards; Henry himself scuffed his shot from a Gilberto pass, and Kiely made superb saves from Wiltord and Edu. More goals would not come, but the Gunners could be well content with an eight-point Premiership lead.

FA Cup Quarter Final
Saturday 8 March 2003 at Highbury, 5.15 p.m.

ARSENAL 2

Jeffers 36, Henry 45

1	David SEAMAN
12	LAUREN
23	Sol CAMPBELL
5	Martin KEOWN
16	Giovanni VAN BRONCKHORST
15	Ray PARLOUR
4	Patrick VIEIRA
17	EDU
8	Fredrik LJUNGBERG
14	Thierry HENRY
9	Francis JEFFERS

Substitutes

20	Guillaume WARMUZ
18	Pascal CYGAN
28	Kolo TOURE (Henry) 78
7	Robert PIRES (Ljungberg) 64
11	Sylvain WILTORD (Jeffers) 64

MATCH REPORT

Arsenal fought back brilliantly from the shock of conceding a soft early goal and seized a seemingly decisive lead, only to be frustrated by valiant Chelsea at the climax of a rousing rollercoaster of a quarter-final.

It was the visitors, looking for their first FA Cup victory over the Gunners in more than half a century, who made the early running, with Keown's slip allowing Zola to advance on Seaman, who blocked his shot.

Less than a minute later Chelsea were in front when a short corner reached Gronkjaer, Arsenal's offside trap failed to function and the winger's cross was headed in from six yards by the unmarked Terry.

At least the hosts had plenty of time to redress the balance and Henry led the charge, out-muscling Gallas and cutting in towards Cudicini, who saved decisively at the Frenchman's feet.

An even better chance materialised after 20 minutes when Jeffers ran on to a Vieira through-ball and sprawled as he attempted to dance past the 'keeper, who rose to make a plunging save from Henry's spot-kick.

Patrick Vieira challenges for midfield possession with his friend and former Arsenal colleague, Emmanuel Petit.

At the other end a Morris miscue was hacked away by Keown, but Arsenal were dominating possession and reaped the benefit when Ljungberg's shot rebounded from Cudicini, Babayaro failed to clear and Jeffers bundled home.

Henry almost put his side ahead when his sidefooted shot rebounded from an upright, then did so when sent clear by Vieira in first-half stoppage

2 CHELSEA

Terry 3, Lampard 84

23	Carlo CUDICINI
15	Mario MELCHIOT
13	William GALLAS
26	John TERRY
3	Celestine BABAYARO
30	Jesper GRONKJAER
8	Frank LAMPARD
17	Emmanuel PETIT
20	Jody MORRIS
25	Gianfranco ZOLA
9	Jimmy Floyd HASSELBAINK

Substitutes

35	Rhys EVANS
29	Robert HUTH
21	Enrique DE LUCAS (Gronkjaer) 72
11	Boudewijn ZENDEN (Zola) 46
22	Eidur GUDJOHNSEN (Petit) 72

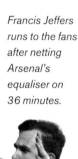

Francis Jeffers runs to the fans after netting Arsenal's equaliser on 36 minutes.

Celestine Babayaro slides in and John Terry (on the line) watches helplessly as Jeffers scores.

time, pirouetting past Cudicini and stroking into the vacant goal.

Though the Gunners continued to be the more fluent team after the break, Chelsea fought courageously and Seaman was forced to save superbly from Hasselbaink, then Gallas missed with a free header before Lampard prodded a late equaliser in a scrimmage following a Zenden corner.

Still there was time for a potent Arsenal riposte, but in the third minute of injury time Cudicini parried an explosive free-kick from van Bronckhorst, and that was that.

BOOKINGS

Arsenal Edu 16
Chelsea Cudicini 20, Morris 30

Thierry Henry's clever turn perplexes Carlo Cudicini, leaving the Chelsea 'keeper facing the wrong way as the ball heads for goal.

UEFA Champions League, Phase Two, Group B
Tuesday 11 March 2003 at Highbury, 7.45 p.m.

ARSENAL 1
Vieira 12

1 David SEAMAN

12 LAUREN

5 Martin KEOWN

18 Pascal CYGAN

16 Giovanni VAN BRONCKHORST

11 Sylvain WILTORD

19 GILBERTO Silva

4 Patrick VIEIRA

7 Robert PIRES

10 Dennis BERGKAMP

14 Thierry HENRY

Substitutes

13 Stuart TAYLOR

26 Igors STEPANOVS

28 Kolo TOURE

15 Ray PARLOUR

8 Fredrik LJUNGBERG (Wiltord) 73

25 Nwankwo KANU (Lauren) 88

9 Francis JEFFERS (Bergkamp) 73

MATCH REPORT

The Gunners were held to a draw as their finishing let them down against ten-man Roma. However, with Ajax and Valencia also drawing in Amsterdam, qualification for the quarter-finals remained in Arsenal's own hands with one group match remaining.

After seizing an early lead through Vieira's soaring header from a van Bronckhorst corner, they created a catalogue of scoring opportunities but spurned them all.

Arsenal served notice of their attacking intentions in the fourth minute when Gilberto's deep cross was met by a Wiltord volley which Pelizzoli turned over the crossbar.

When Totti was dismissed for catching Keown with a flailing arm it seemed that the Romans must crumble, but Pelizzoli saved a free-kick from Henry and a low shot from Wiltord, and when he was beaten by a Pires nod the strike was ruled out for offside.

The picture changed in first-half stoppage time when, in Roma's first meaningful raid of the night, Cassano lost his

Robert Pires gets under the ball as Christian Panucci looks on.

Patrick Vieira rises above Roma's Aldair to send a soaring header past Roma 'keeper Ivan Pelizzoli.

1 ROMA

Cassano 45

22	Ivan PELIZZOLI
23	Christian PANUCCI
6	Dos Santos ALDAIR
19	Walter SAMUEL
2	Marcos CAFU
17	Damiano TOMMASI
11	Fereira EMERSON
8	Francisco LIMA
32	Vincent CANDELA
10	Francesco TOTTI
18	Antonio CASSANO

Substitutes

1	Francesco ANTONIOLI
4	Luigi SARTOR
13	Leandro CUFRE
7	Diego FUSER
27	Daniele DE ROSSI
25	Gianni GUIGOU
9	Vincenzo MONTELLA
	(Cassano) 62

Top *Sylvain Wiltord runs at the heart of the Roma defence.*
Above *Patrick Vieira shows his delight at opening the scoring after 12 minutes at Highbury.*

markers to race on to a raking pass from Emerson, moving wide of Seaman with his first touch and netting simply with his second.

After the break the Gunners laid siege to Pelizzoli's goal, but the Roma 'keeper saved brilliantly from Wiltord and competently from Pires, then Wiltord, Pires and Henry all fired high from favourable positions in the space of a minute.

Later Keown nodded into Pelizzoli's arms and Gilberto shaved an upright with a sudden venomous drive, but it was Roma who went closest to sealing the points in the 85th minute when Cafu charged down the right flank and crossed to the unmarked Montella, who headed over from six yards.

BOOKINGS

Arsenal van Bronckhorst 29
Roma Cassano 28, Samuel 32, Aldair 67

DISMISSALS

Roma Totti 22

FA Barclaycard Premiership
Saturday 15 March 2003 at Ewood Park, 3 p.m.

BLACKBURN ROVERS 2

Duff 22, Tugay 52

1	Brad Friedel
21	Martin TAYLOR
25	Henning BERG
6	Craig SHORT
26	Vratislav GRESKO
18	Keith GILLESPIE
7	Garry FLITCROFT
3	Kerimoglu TUGAY
11	Damien DUFF
33	Hakan SUKUR
19	Dwight YORKE

Substitutes

13	Alan KELLY
14	Nils-Eric JOHANSSON (Duff) 69
29	Jon DOUGLAS
12	Corrado GRABBI
31	Paul GALLAGHER (Yorke) 78

Below, left *Blackburn's Vratislav Gresko gets across to block a shot from Freddie Ljungberg.*
Below, right *Ray Parlour tangles with Rovers defender Craig Short.*

MATCH REPORT

Blackburn completed a League double over injury-stricken Arsenal, who suffered their first reverse in 21 games and saw their lead at the Premiership summit cut to two points. Already deprived of Vieira, Seaman, Campbell and Cole, the Gunners lost Keown with a hamstring strain after 18 minutes, and thereafter they were sorely stretched by their enterprising opponents, whose victory was wholly deserved.

Before the exit of Keown, who was replaced in central defence by Gilberto, the visitors had held their own and threatened with two free-kicks; first a curler from Henry demanded a flying save by the impressive Friedel, then a van Bronckhorst daisy-cutter almost sneaked through.

But it was Rovers who took the lead when Tugay's shot rebounded from Sukur and the loose ball landed at the feet of Duff, who volleyed past Taylor from ten yards.

Now Blackburn grew in authority and Gillespie, who had already menaced the left flank of Arsenal's defence, found Duff, whose crisp half-volley from the edge of the box was turned away athletically by Taylor.

0 ARSENAL

	13 Stuart TAYLOR
	12 LAUREN
	5 Martin KEOWN
	18 Pascal CYGAN
	16 Giovanni VAN BRONCKHORST
	8 Fredrik LJUNGBERG
	15 Ray PARLOUR
	17 EDU
	7 Robert PIRES
	10 Dennis BERGKAMP
	14 Thierry HENRY

Substitutes

	20 Guillaume WARMUZ
	28 Kolo TOURE
	19 GILBERTO Silva (Keown) 18
	11 Sylvain WILTORD (Pires) 69
	9 Francis JEFFERS (Edu) 69

Right *Blackburn's Garry Flitcroft slides in to halt the advancing Robert Pires.*
Below *Pires fires a shot wide on a frustrating afternoon for the Gunners at Ewood Park.*

A corner by Henry produced the Gunners' best scoring opportunity of the half, but Pires could not direct his header as the ball bobbled awkwardly in the goalmouth.

BOOKINGS

Blackburn Duff 16, Tugay 31, Flitcroft 48, Sukur 88
Arsenal Parlour 53, van Bronckhorst 76

Rovers continued in the ascendancy after the break and increased their advantage when Duff passed square to Tugay, who carried the ball forward as Cygan backed off, then drilled a low 20-yarder inside Taylor's far post.

Yorke might have put the result beyond reasonable doubt, but he headed past the angle of post and bar from a Gillespie cross, after which Arsenal mounted a period of late pressure.

Bergkamp combined neatly with Henry but Ljungberg shot high, then Short blocked Jeffers after an exquisite turn and pass by Henry. Still nothing would fall the Gunners' way and Arsène Wenger admitted afterwards that it had not been 'the real Arsenal' on display – but he predicted a rapid recovery.

VALENCIA 2

Carew 34, 57

1 Santiago CANIZARES
33 Anthony REVEILLERE
4 Roberto AYALA
2 Mauricio PELLEGRINO
15 Amedeo CARBONI
19 Francisco RUFETE
6 David ALBELDA
21 Pablo AIMAR
14 Rodrigues VICENTE
11 Juan SANCHEZ
7 John CAREW

Substitutes

13 Andres PALOP (Canizares) 71
3 Fabio AURELIO
5 Miroslav DJUKIC
12 Carlos MARCHENA (Carew) 89
10 Miguel ANGULO (Sanchez) 68
20 Miguel MISTA
22 Gonzalo DE LOS SANTOS

Thierry Henry curls home a shot that puts Arsenal back in the game after 49 minutes.

MATCH REPORT

The Gunners' Champions League road ended frustratingly in Valencia. After making a dashing start, with four goal attempts in the opening eight minutes, Arsène Wenger's men were contained by the Spanish Champions and finally put to the sword by Carew, the same striker whose goal had knocked them out of the competition two years earlier.

Henry demonstrated Arsenal's positive intentions with a first-minute shot from the right angle of Valencia's box which demanded a smart save from Canizares. Soon Pires had fired into the side netting and Henry had been foiled twice more as the visitors continued to surge forward with zest.

They went agonisingly close to taking a deserved lead after 29 minutes when Gilberto met Henry's corner with a thunderous header, but the ball hit Vicente, cannoned on to the underside of the crossbar and was scrambled clear.

Valencia appeared to take heart from their narrow escape, however, and they went ahead when Carew latched on to a clever pass from Aimar and cracked a low shot past Taylor from 18 yards.

Arsenal resumed their offensive after the break, with Henry curling a free-kick narrowly wide, then scoring a brilliant equaliser when he raced on to a measured through-ball from Pires and bent an unerring shot around the advancing Canizares.

The Spaniards hit back spiritedly, and Taylor plunged athletically to divert a Carew header from a Vicente cross, only to be undone by an identical combination

1 ARSENAL

Henry 49

13	Stuart TAYLOR
12	LAUREN
23	Sol CAMPBELL
18	Pascal CYGAN
28	Kolo TOURE
11	Sylvain WILTORD
19	GILBERTO Silva
4	Patrick VIEIRA
8	Fredrik LJUNGBERG
7	Robert PIRES
14	Thierry HENRY

Substitutes

41	Craig HOLLOWAY
26	Igors STEPANOVS
16	Giovanni VAN BRONCKHORST
15	Ray PARLOUR
17	EDU
25	Nwankwo KANU (Toure) 86
9	Francis JEFFERS (Wiltord) 76

Right *Freddie Ljungberg attempts to stride through the heart of the Valencia defence.*

Below, right *Patrick Vieira wins possession in midfield.*

after Gilberto had conceded possession a minute later.

The Arsenal 'keeper averted further damage with a fine save from a towering header by Ayala and a courageous dive at the feet of the charging Carew, but late efforts by Wiltord and Henry could not force the point needed to secure a quarter-final place.

BOOKINGS

Valencia Carboni 36, Pellegrino 54, Aimar 76

Arsenal Vieira 42, Pires 90

FA Barclaycard Premiership
Sunday 23 March 2003 at Highbury, 4.05 p.m.

ARSENAL 2

Cygan 8, Vieira 64

13 Stuart TAYLOR
12 LAUREN
23 Sol CAMPBELL
18 Pascal CYGAN
16 Giovanni VAN BRONCKHORST
8 Fredrik LJUNGBERG
19 GILBERTO Silva
4 Patrick VIEIRA
7 Robert PIRES
10 Dennis BERGKAMP
14 Thierry HENRY

Substitutes

20 Guillaume WARMUZ
28 Kolo TOURE (Bergkamp) 79
15 Ray PARLOUR (Pires) 68
11 Sylvain WILTORD
9 Francis JEFFERS

Below, left *Thomas Gravesen hauls down Dennis Bergkamp.*
Below, right *Robert Pires congratulates goalscorer Pascal Cygan.*

MATCH REPORT

Having conceded their long-held Premiership lead some 24 hours earlier, Arsenal leapfrogged Manchester United and went back to the top thanks to a hard-earned victory over Everton.

The Gunners started fluently and they grabbed an early advantage when Cygan scored his first goal for the club, the French defender glancing home a header from Henry's corner.

A second almost materialised when Vieira fed Bergkamp and the Dutchman's low shot was spilled by Wright, but the former Arsenal 'keeper made amends with a brave plunge at the feet of Henry. Bergkamp went close three times in the space of four minutes midway through the half, forcing Wright to save twice and scraping an upright with a 25-yard volley following an extravagant flick.

But Everton showed signs of enterprise as the interval approached, with Rooney setting up chances which Gravesen and Pembridge could not take. They continued to press forward after the break, with former Gunner Kevin

1   EVERTON

Rooney 56

1	Richard WRIGHT
20	Joseph YOBO
5	David WEIR
4	Alan STUBBS
6	David UNSWORTH
2	Steve WATSON
16	Thomas GRAVESEN
12	Li TIE
11	Mark PEMBRIDGE
9	Kevin CAMPBELL
18	Wayne ROONEY

Substitutes

13	Steve SIMONSEN
15	Gary NAYSMITH
17	Scot GEMMILL (Tie) 74
26	Lee CARSLEY
10	Duncan FERGUSON (Watson) 79

Campbell shooting into Taylor's side-netting after a Rooney pull-back.

The threat from England's youngest international was clear, and three minutes later he scored a superb equaliser, receiving a pass from Campbell on the right flank, then dispatching a low cross-shot from the edge of the box through the legs of the retreating Cygan.

In the next move Rooney was off target with a snap-shot, but the mounting tension around Highbury was eased when Henry nodded into the Everton box, Bergkamp and Unsworth tussled and the ball ran free to Vieira who hammered it into the net from six yards.

After their second strike, the Gunners mounted steady pressure, and they seemed on the point of a third goal when Henry touched back to Ljungberg, who burst between two defenders only to thrash his shot high over the bar from an acute angle.

Ferguson, Everton's combative substitute, won a few late headers but not in the danger area, and Arsenal eased over the finishing line.

BOOKINGS

Arsenal Lauren 52, Henry 87
Everton Tie 62

Above, left *Patrick Vieira lashes home the winning goal after good work from Dennis Bergkamp.*
Above, right *Ray Parlour makes progress down the right flank despite the unwanted attention of Everton's David Unsworth.*

105

FA Cup 6th Round Replay
Tuesday 25 March 2003 at Stamford Bridge, 7.45 p.m.

CHELSEA 1

Terry 79

23 Carlo CUDICINI
15 Mario MELCHIOT
26 John TERRY
13 William GALLAS
12 Mario STANIC
8 Frank LAMPARD
20 Jody MORRIS
17 Emmanuel PETIT
14 Graeme LE SAUX
25 Gianfranco ZOLA
9 Jimmy Floyd HASSELBAINK

Substitutes
1 Ed DE GOEY
6 Marcel DESAILLY
30 Jesper GRONKJAER (Stanic) 35
11 Boudewijn ZENDEN (Morris) 46
22 Eidur GUDJOHNSEN (Petit) 59

Below, left *Lauren, scorer of Arsenal's third goal, lets fly from the edge of the box.*
Below, right *Stuart Taylor leads the post-match applause accompanied by Jeffers (left) and Ljungberg (right).*

MATCH REPORT

Arsenal knocked Chelsea out of the FA Cup for the third successive season, thanks to a valiant display at Stamford Bridge. Furthermore, with Leeds beaten by Sheffield United, the Gunners were one of only two Premiership clubs left in the competition.

The Blues poured forward relentlessly for much of the first half and almost all the second, but the visitors defended strongly and punished their London rivals on the break. Arsenal heroes abounded, but particular praise should be reserved for Taylor, who made a string of crucial saves, and the mighty Vieira, who shrugged off the effects of a knee injury with a performance that was inspirational.

Chelsea began forcefully and missed an early chance when Hasselbaink's free header from a Le Saux corner bounced over the crossbar. Taylor saved smartly from Lampard, but for all the Blues' territorial advantage, the Gunners were passing more incisively and soon they made it pay. Wiltord sprinted through the centre and found Vieira on the right, the skipper delivered a low cross and Terry miskicked past Cudicini from six yards.

As the hosts retaliated, Taylor turned over a deflected free-kick by Hasselbaink, but then the visitors launched another devastating counter-attack, Vieira carrying the ball from deep

3 ARSENAL

Terry og 24, Wiltord 34, Lauren 82

before slipping it to Wiltord, who rifled past Cudicini form 12 yards.

After the break Chelsea mounted a siege, with Taylor saving from Petit's overhead and Gronkjaer's drive, and when Gudjohnsen did find the net he was flagged offside.

The assault intensified after Cygan's red card and finally the Blues broke through when Terry stooped to nod home from a Hasselbaink cross. But their hopes of resurrection were shortlived, as Lauren broke away on the right and cut past two defenders before beating Cudicini at his near post from 16 yards.

Even then Chelsea refused to submit, and the Arsenal 'keeper saved brilliantly from Gudjohnsen (twice) and Hasselbaink before a semi-final berth was confirmed.

13	Stuart TAYLOR
12	LAUREN
23	Sol CAMPBELL
18	Pascal CYGAN
28	Kolo TOURE
15	Ray PARLOUR
4	Patrick VIEIRA
17	EDU
7	Robert PIRES
11	Sylvain WILTORD
9	Francis JEFFERS

Substitutes

20	Guillaume WARMUZ
16	Giovanni VAN BRONCKHORST (Jeffers) 68
8	Fredrik LJUNGBERG (Pires) 74
10	Dennis BERGKAMP
14	Thierry HENRY (Wiltord) 75

BOOKINGS

Chelsea Stanic 17
Arsenal Cygan 31, Lauren 81

DISMISSAL

Arsenal Cygan 66

FA Barclaycard Premiership	25 March 2003	P	W	D	L	F	A	Pts
ARSENAL		31	20	6	5	66	33	66
Manchester United		31	19	7	5	51	27	64
Newcastle United		31	19	4	8	54	35	61
Chelsea		31	15	9	7	57	31	54
Liverpool		31	14	10	7	47	31	52
Everton		31	14	8	9	39	36	50
Charlton Athletic		31	13	7	11	40	39	46
Blackburn Rovers		31	12	10	9	38	37	46
Southampton		31	11	11	9	34	32	44
Tottenham Hotspur		31	12	7	12	43	44	43
Middlesbrough		31	11	9	11	39	35	42
Manchester City		31	12	5	14	40	49	41
Fulham		31	10	8	13	35	40	38
Aston Villa		31	10	6	15	33	37	36
Birmingham City		31	9	8	14	28	42	35
Leeds United		31	10	4	17	38	45	34
Bolton Wanderers		31	7	11	13	34	47	32
West Ham United		31	7	9	15	34	53	30
West Bromwich Albion		31	5	6	20	21	47	21
Sunderland		31	4	7	20	19	50	19

Above, left *Sylvain Wiltord scored the all important second goal against the Blues.*

107

ASTON VILLA 1

Toure og 71

1 Peter ENCKELMAN
4 Olof MELLBERG
27 Ronny JOHNSEN
6 Gareth BARRY
15 Ulises DE LA CRUZ
23 Joey GUDJONSSON
17 Lee HENDRIE
12 Tomas HITZLSPERGER
21 J Lloyd SAMUEL
20 Mustapha HADJI
10 Darius VASSELL

Substitutes

13 Stefan POSTMA
30 Rob EDWARDS (De La Cruz) 66
28 Oyvind LEONHARDSEN (Hadji) 79
14 Marcus ALLBACK (Gudjonsson) 66
25 Stefan MOORE

Below, left *Dennis Bergkamp controls the ball under the watchful eye of Villa's Gareth Barry.*

Below, right *Lauren has eyes only for the ball despite Mustapha Hadji's challenge.*

MATCH REPORT

Arsenal's advantage at the top of the Premiership was trimmed to goal difference as they were frustrated by well-drilled and disciplined opponents for long periods of a mundane encounter.

Bergkamp made an early attempt to pick his way through Villa's densely populated midfield, but his run past four tackles was halted, then Barry responded with a shot which cleared Taylor's goal and landed in the Holt End. Graham Taylor's men fashioned a clearer opening when De La Cruz intercepted a Campbell clearance and crossed to Hadji, but the Moroccan miscued with a volley from ten yards.

Arsenal closed the first half on the offensive when Ljungberg brought a decent save from Enckelman, and Henry began the second with a spectacular volley which landed on the roof of Villa's net. Now the Champions were in their stride, but a Vieira shot was deflected wide, then Henry's cross-goal dispatch eluded Ljungberg at full stretch.

The mounting pressure finally told when Bergkamp located Gilberto on the right and the Brazilian's shot was

1 ARSENAL

Ljungberg 56

13	Stuart TAYLOR
12	LAUREN
23	Sol CAMPBELL
18	Pascal CYGAN
28	Kolo TOURE
15	Ray PARLOUR
19	GILBERTO Silva
4	Patrick VIEIRA
8	Fredrik LJUNGBERG
10	Dennis BERGKAMP
14	Thierry HENRY

Substitutes

20	Guillaume WARMUZ
78	Ashley COLE (Toure) 78
17	EDU
11	Sylvain WILTORD (Parlour) 79
9	Francis JEFFERS (Bergkamp) 85

Left *Ljungberg flicks a shot goalward.*

Below *Enckelman's dive forces Vieira wide.*

repelled by Enckelman to the feet of Ljungberg, who tucked the ball home from six yards.

Thus forced to go forward, Villa retaliated with a 20-yard scorcher from Hitzlsperger which was tipped over deftly by Taylor and a fierce Johnsen effort was blocked. Still the Gunners looked reasonably comfortable, but there was no legislating for the bizarre nature of the equaliser.

A Hitzlsperger corner from the right caused confusion in the Arsenal box, Cygan could not control the bouncing ball, and Toure, attempting to clear from under the crossbar, lashed high into his own net.

Thereafter Arsenal made a succession of late efforts to restore their lead, and one penetrating run by Wiltord was thwarted only by a last-ditch challenge from Samuel.

Yet as stoppage time ticked away it was Aston Villa on the front foot, and the Gunners were forced to settle for a point.

BOOKINGS

Aston Villa Allback 81
Arsenal Vieira 23, Jeffers 87

ARSENAL 1

Ljungberg 34

1 David SEAMAN

12 LAUREN

5 Martin KEOWN

23 Sol CAMPBELL

3 Ashley COLE

15 Ray PARLOUR

4 Patrick VIEIRA

17 EDU

8 Fredrik LJUNGBERG

11 Sylvain WILTORD

9 Francis JEFFERS

Substitutes

13 Stuart TAYLOR

22 Oleg LUZHNY

19 GILBERTO Silva (Vieira) 56

10 Dennis BERGKAMP (Wiltord) 81

14 Thierry HENRY (Jeffers) 66

MATCH REPORT

Arsenal never touched their majestic best, but edged into their third successive FA Cup final thanks to a solitary, hotly disputed first-half strike by Freddie Ljungberg.

The most memorable moment of an attritional contest, though, featured David Seaman, who celebrated his 1,000th senior match with a phenomenal late save which ensured the Gunners' progress to the Millennium Stadium in May.

The earlier controversy involved a tackle from Campbell which left Allison on the ground, then an inadvertent body-check on Tonge by referee Graham Poll as Arsenal's subsequent match-winning move developed.

Eventually Ljungberg dinked deftly to Jeffers, who scampered to the left byline and crossed low to Wiltord; the Frenchman nudged his first shot against the far post, then he retrieved possession and tried again, the ball falling to Ljungberg who netted via the crossbar from seven yards.

Soon afterwards Edu went close to doubling the lead but his free-kick whistled narrowly wide of Kenny's upright. Still, United were far from finished as an attacking force and after the break Ndlovu might have equalised, but he fired straight at Seaman.

Gradually the game became more open and there were good opportunities for Wiltord at one end and Brown at the other, then the Blades' Curtis lifted an effort over the bar.

Below, left *In the right place at the right time again… Freddie Ljungberg fires home the decisive goal.*
Below, right *David Seaman keeps out Paul Peschisolido's late header with a truly remarkable save.*

Attendance 59,170
Referee Graham Poll

0 SHEFFIELD UNITED

23 Patrick KENNY
36 John CURTIS
2 Robert KOZLUK
6 Robert PAGE
17 Phil JAGIELKA
7 Michael BROWN
8 Stuart McCALL
18 Michael TONGE
16 Peter NDLOVU
34 Steve KABBA
14 Wayne ALLISON

Substitutes

24 Gary KELLY
5 Shaun MURPHY
12 Nick MONTGOMERY (Allison) 60
9 Carl ASABA (McCall) 60
10 Paul PESCHISOLIDO (Kabba) 79

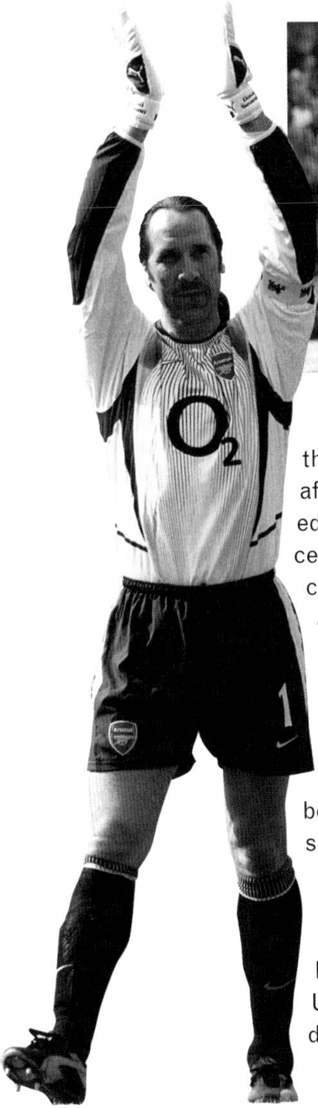

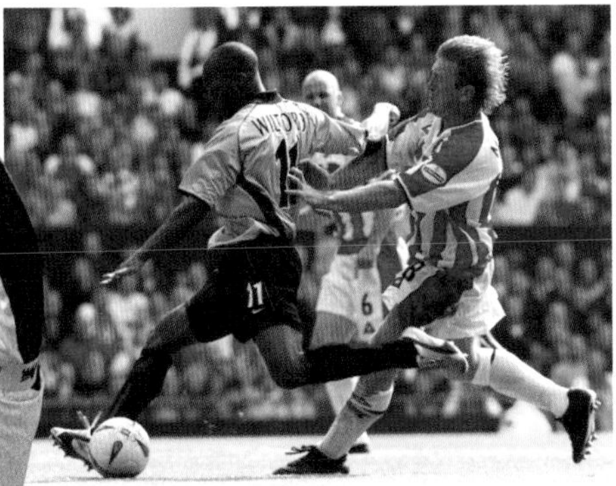

Arsenal might have sealed the spoils through both Henry and Ljungberg, but after 84 minutes they were deeply indebted to Seaman for preventing a seemingly certain leveller. Tonge delivered a deep corner from the right, Page nodded back across the box and Asaba miscued wildly with a close-range volley. However, the loose ball arced to Peschisolido, who headed past the England goalkeeper from three yards; somehow David clawed the ball back before it crossed the line and Jagielka skied the rebound high into the crowd.

As the final whistle approached, Arsène Wenger's men looked the more likely scorers, with Bergkamp and Henry exploiting the space left as United pushed forward with increasing desperation.

BOOKINGS

Arsenal Cole 30

Sheffield United McCall 25, Brown 48, Asaba 71

Above, right *Stuart McCall takes desperate action to halt the run of Sylvain Wiltord.*
Above, left *David Seaman acknowledges the crowd on the occasion of his 1,000th senior career appearance.*

ARSENAL 2

Henry 51, 62

13	Stuart TAYLOR
12	LAUREN
5	Martin KEOWN
23	Sol CAMPBELL
3	Ashley COLE
8	Fredrik LJUNGBERG
19	GILBERTO Silva
4	Patrick VIEIRA
7	Robert PIRES
10	Dennis BERGKAMP
14	Thierry HENRY

Substitutes

20	Guillaume WARMUZ
22	Oleg LUZHNY
17	EDU (Vieira) 34
11	Sylvain WILTORD (Bergkamp) 75
25	Nwankwo KANU (Pires) 80

MATCH REPORT

Title rivals Arsenal and Manchester United shared the points on a night of high drama that was soured by the late, controversial dismissal of Sol Campbell.

Both sides might have claimed victory, with the visitors contending that the Gunners' second goal was struck from a seemingly offside position, while the hosts pointed out that Thierry Henry was within an ace of volleying a stoppage-time winner, only to be foiled by the legs of Fabien Barthez.

After a frenetically nervous start, United were the first to settle and Scholes missed a golden opportunity to open the scoring when he mis-headed a Solskjaer cross.

The next chance, too, fell to the blue-shirted visitors, this time van Nistelrooy dinking marginally high after O'Shea's pass was flicked on by Scholes, but the Dutchman made no mistake three minutes later. After a neat interchange with Giggs, he turned past Campbell, eluded Keown and lifted the ball over the advancing Taylor.

By then Arsenal's inspirational skipper, Vieira, was labouring with a knee injury, yet after his departure the Gunners rallied bravely and Ljungberg almost grabbed an equaliser shortly before the break.

The contest was transformed early in the second half when Cole battled past two challenges and his scuffed shot rebounded from the back of Henry's legs before screwing past Barthez in the United goal.

Now there was a new spring in Arsenal's step and they capitalised when Cole found

United's Rio Ferdinand goes to ground in his efforts to dispossess Thierry Henry.

2 MANCHESTER UNITED

van Nistelrooy 24, Giggs 63

1	Fabien BARTHEZ
24	Wesley BROWN
6	Rio FERDINAND
27	Mikael SILVESTRE
22	John O'SHEA
20	Ole Gunnar SOLSKJAER
8	Nicky BUTT
16	Roy KEANE
11	Ryan GIGGS
18	Paul SCHOLES
10	Ruud VAN NISTELROOY

Substitutes

19	RICARDO
2	Gary NEVILLE (O'Shea) 46
3	Phil NEVILLE
7	David BECKHAM
21	Diego FORLAN

Henry beyond United's back line; there was no flag and the Frenchman strode on to secure the lead with a neat finish.

However, Sir Alex Ferguson's men levelled almost instantly when Solskjaer swung over a dispatch from the right and the unmarked Giggs beat Taylor with a downward header.

Thereafter the action switched from end to end before boiling over when Campbell's arm contacted Solskjaer's face and the England stopper was shown the red card. Even then, the ten men of Arsenal almost prevailed, but it was not to be.

BOOKINGS

Manchester United Keane 47, Butt 80

DISMISSALS

Arsenal Campbell 82

Above, left *Henry and Cole drop to their knees in celebration.*
Above, right *Robert Pires attempts to hurdle Wes Brown's sliding challenge.*

FA Barclaycard Premiership
Saturday 19 April 2003 at The Riverside, 3 p.m.

MIDDLESBROUGH   0

1	Mark SCHWARZER
28	Colin COOPER
4	Ugo EHIOGU
6	Gareth SOUTHGATE
3	Franck QUEUDRUE
7	George BOATENG
20	Guidoni DORIVA
10	JUNINHO
12	Jonathan GREENING
8	Szilard NEMETH
19	Malcolm CHRISTIE

Substitutes

35	Bradley JONES
2	Robbie STOCKDALE
31	Luke WILKSHIRE (Doriva) 69
16	Joseph-Desire JOB (Christie) 82
9	Massimo MACCARONE (Juninho) 82

Below, left *Team-mates descend upon Thierry Henry as he celebrates scoring Arsenal's second goal.*
Below, right *Freddie Ljungberg breaks forward at pace.*

MATCH REPORT

The Gunners displayed class and character aplenty as they inflicted a rare home defeat on Middlesbrough It was also a victory that recharged Arsenal's momentum in the race for the Championship.

Inspired yet again by the irrepressible Thierry Henry, they made light of the absence through injury of Patrick Vieira, for whom Ray Parlour deputised imperiously, and controlled lengthy swathes of the action.

However, it was Boro who showed the earliest attacking ambition when Juninho made space on the left, only for his cross to be headed wide by Christie. Henry responded with a shot which was blocked, then an audacious backheel to Wiltord, whose threat was quelled by a Southgate intervention.

The only persistent menace to Arsenal emanated from Juninho's astute passing, but when his pass reached Christie shortly before the interval, Taylor saved courageously at the marksman's feet.

The Gunners imposed their authority on proceedings three

2 ARSENAL

Wiltord 48, Henry 82

13	Stuart TAYLOR
12	LAUREN
23	Sol CAMPBELL
18	Pascal CYGAN
3	Ashley COLE
8	Fredrik LJUNGBERG
19	GILBERTO Silva
15	Ray PARLOUR
7	Robert PIRES
11	Sylvain WILTORD
14	Thierry HENRY

Substitutes

20	Guillaume WARMUZ
5	Martin KEOWN
22	Oleg LUZHNY (Cole) 83
16	Giovanni VAN BRONCKHORST (Pires) 90
10	Dennis BERGKAMP (Henry) 88

minutes into the second period when Henry dispossessed Doriva on the right, then found Wiltord, who netted beautifully with a low, first-time 15-yarder, his first Premiership strike for five months.

Now the hosts countered penetratingly but when Nemeth's probing cross from the left dropped to Greening, he miskicked wildly. For Arsenal Ljungberg played in Wiltord on the right, but the Frenchman pulled his shot beyond the far post, then Henry set up a tap-in for Cole, only for the England defender to be ruled marginally offside.

Still Boro buzzed forward but the Gunners' rearguard was rarely disturbed until a long ball from Cooper was nodded down to Juninho, who volleyed high from 12 yards.

A second Arsenal goal was needed to settle the issue, and duly it was supplied by Henry, who stroked home a trademark curling free-kick from the left corner of the box after Cole had been felled in full flight by Boateng.

After that, Steve McLaren's men made a late damage-limitation bid, but an Ehiogu shot rebounded away off Ljungberg and Queudrue's fierce free-kick cleared the crossbar.

BOOKINGS

Arsenal Henry 42

Above, left *Robert Pires pursues the celebrating Sylvain Wiltord.*
Above, right *Ray Parlour acknowledges the travelling Arsenal fans at The Riverside.*

BOLTON WANDERERS   2

Djorkaeff 74, Keown og 83

22	Jussi JAASKELAINEN
4	Gudni BERGSSON
17	Florent LAVILLE
5	Bruno N'GOTTY
2	Bernard MENDY
16	Ivan CAMPO
8	Per FRANDSEN
10	Jay-Jay OKOCHA
11	Ricardo GARDNER
13	Youri DJORKAEFF
9	Henrik PEDERSEN

Substitutes

30	Kevin POOLE
25	Simon CHARLTON
15	Kevin NOLAN (Campo) 72
18	Pierre-Yves ANDRE (Mendy) 72
20	Ballesta SALVA (Pedersen) 83

MATCH REPORT

After soon-to-be-crowned PFA player of the season Thierry Henry had demonstrated his quality yet again, fashioning chances which were converted by Sylvain Wiltord and Robert Pires, the Gunners were poised on the brink of returning to the Premiership pinnacle. But then they surrendered two late goals to Bolton and the destiny of the title moved out of their hands.

Arsenal had begun purposefully and might have seized an early initiative when Parlour dispossessed Campo and fed Henry, but the Frenchman's flashing cross from the left eluded his charging team-mates.

The Trotters responded gamely and Pedersen's shot on the turn shaved a post, but gradually the Gunners asserted themselves, with Henry looking increasingly unstoppable. First he almost put in Wiltord, then he found Ljungberg, whose 20-yarder demanded a plunging dive from Jaaskelainen, and next he drew a save from the 'keeper with a low drive.

After the interval, though, Henry was not to be denied, leaving several defenders in his wake as he scampered down the left before cutting inside to lay on a comfortable tap-in for Wiltord.

Seaman prevented an equaliser with an acrobatic scoop to repel a looping Frandsen header before the Champions moved further ahead in style. Henry accepted a pass from Cole on the left, then beat two defenders with a trade-mark body-swerve and touched to Pires, who sent an imperious 20-

Sylvain Witord leaps over the diving Jussi Jaaskelainen after netting the game's opening goal.

2 ARSENAL

Wiltord 47, Pires 56

1	David SEAMAN
12	LAUREN
23	Sol CAMPBELL
18	Pascal CYGAN
3	Ashley COLE
8	Fredrik LJUNGBERG
19	GILBERTO Silva
15	Ray PARLOUR
7	Robert PIRES
11	Sylvain WILTORD
14	Thierry HENRY

Substitutes

13	Stuart TAYLOR
5	Martin KEOWN (Cygan) 67
22	Oleg LUZHNY (Ljungberg) 58
16	Giovanni VAN BRONCKHORST (Lauren) 72
10	Dennis BERGKAMP

yard curler beyond Jaaskelainen.

But Bolton refused to yield, Djorkaeff tucking neatly past Seaman after a Frandsen drive had rebounded from an upright. Thereafter the England 'keeper foiled Pedersen twice, but he was helpless to intervene when Djorkaeff swung over a free-kick from the left and the ball glanced off Keown's head on the way into the net. Even six minutes of stoppage time, caused by a rash of Arsenal injuries, were not enough to produce a winner.

BOOKINGS

Bolton Wanderers Laville 31, Campo 60
Arsenal Henry 33, Parlour 80

DISMISSALS

Bolton Wanderers Laville 90

FA Barclaycard Premiership	26 April 2003						
	P	W	D	L	F	A	Pts
Manchester United	35	22	8	5	66	32	74
ARSENAL	35	21	9	5	73	38	72
Newcastle United	36	20	5	11	60	46	65
Chelsea	36	18	10	8	66	36	64
Liverpool	36	18	10	8	59	37	64
Everton	36	17	8	11	47	45	59
Blackburn Rovers	36	15	11	10	47	42	56
Tottenham Hotspur	35	14	8	13	50	51	50
Charlton Athletic	36	14	7	15	44	51	49
Southampton	35	12	12	11	41	40	48
Manchester City	35	14	6	15	45	51	48
Birmingham City	36	13	8	15	39	46	47
Middlesbrough	36	12	10	14	42	41	46
Aston Villa	36	11	9	16	40	44	42
Fulham	36	11	9	16	38	50	42
Leeds United	36	12	5	19	52	54	41
Bolton Wanderers	36	9	13	14	39	50	40
West Ham United	35	8	11	16	38	57	35
West Bromwich Albion	36	6	6	24	26	62	24
Sunderland	36	4	7	25	21	60	19

Robert Pires challenges Bolton's Ricardo Gardner.

ARSENAL 2

Henry 30, Bergkamp 63

1 David SEAMAN

28 Kolo TOURE

5 Martin KEOWN

22 Oleg LUZHNY

3 Ashley COLE

11 Sylvain WILTORD

19 GILBERTO Silva

15 Ray PARLOUR

7 Robert PIRES

10 Dennis BERGKAMP

14 Thierry HENRY

Substitutes

13 Stuart TAYLOR

26 Igors STEPANOVS

16 Giovanni VAN BRONCKHORST
   (Pires) 80

21 Jermaine PENNANT (Wiltord) 76

25 Nwankwo KANU (Toure) 70

Below, left *Thierry Henry is on hand to nod home after Ray Parlour's long-distance shot comes back off the crossbar.*

Below, right *Parlour tussles with Leeds' Gary Kelly.*

MATCH REPORT

Confronted by a side battling desperately for Premiership survival, Arsène Wenger's under-strength Gunners fought back twice after going behind and fashioned enough chances to win several games. However, they were denied repeatedly by the woodwork, then punished cruelly by a contentious late Leeds winner.

The frustration commenced in the third minute when Gilberto thumped the Yorkshiremen's crossbar with a header from a Pires corner. Then the visitors took the lead in spectacular fashion, Kewell racing on to a raking pass from Wilcox and netting with a searing cross-shot from 25 yards.

Briefly Arsenal were stunned, and Leeds might have extended their advantage, but Kewell hit the side-netting after rounding Seaman and Viduka dinked into the 'keeper's hands from six yards.

But the Gunners showed admirable resilience and when Parlour's 30-yard drive was turned against the bar by Robinson, Henry was on hand to nod in the rebound.

Now the force was with the hosts, but another Parlour effort was hacked off the line by Duberry and Wiltord was ruled offside when he volleyed home after Henry had struck an upright from 30 yards.

3 LEEDS UNITED

Kewell 5, Harte 49, Viduka 88

13	Paul ROBINSON
18	Danny MILLS
22	Michael DUBERRY
5	Lucas RADEBE
3	Ian HARTE
2	Gary KELLY
19	Eirik BAKKE
21	Dominic MATTEO
16	Jason WILCOX
10	Harry KEWELL
9	Mark VIDUKA

Substitutes

1	Nigel MARTYN
11	Raul BRAVO
12	Nick BARMBY
38	James MILNER
39	Simon JOHNSON (Kewell) 80

Left *Sylvain Wiltord takes on a Leeds defender.*

Below *Robert Pires carries the ball forward as the Gunners go in search of a late goal.*

BOOKINGS

Arsenal Bergkamp 65, Keown 90
Leeds United Viduka 66

Shortly after the break Leeds defied the run of play to nose ahead once more when Harte's free-kick took deflections off both Cole and Gilberto to nestle inside Seaman's far post.

Arsenal retaliated with wave after wave of attacks, which finally bore fruit when Pires cut in from the left and found Bergkamp, who stabbed in from six yards.

Thereafter the Champions continued to mount virtually incessant pressure, and Henry went agonisingly close with a brilliant long-range curler that bounced to safety off the foot of a post.

But as time ebbed away, Matteo fed Viduka, who charged through to shoot past Seaman from a seemingly offside position. The flag remained down and Arsenal's hopes of retaining their Championship were dead.

ARSENAL 6

Pires 9, 22, 47, Pennant 15, 18, 25

13	Stuart TAYLOR
28	Kolo TOURE
22	Oleg LUZHNY
26	Igors STEPANOVS
40	Ryan GARRY
21	Jermaine PENNANT
15	Ray PARLOUR
16	Giovanni VAN BRONCKHORST
7	Robert PIRES
25	Nwankwo KANU
14	Thierry HENRY

Substitutes

20	Guillaume WARMUZ
27	Stathis TAVLARIDIS (Luzhny) 75
42	Justin HOYTE (Pennant) 89
10	Dennis BERGKAMP (Pires) 61
11	Sylvain WILTORD

Below *Robert Pires celebrates with the Arsenal supporters after one of his three goals against Saints.*
Right *The French midfielder saved his best for last, completing his hat-trick with a deft chip from outside the box.*

MATCH REPORT

The rampant Gunners shrugged off their title disappointment in rousing style by slamming Southampton, their FA Cup Final opponents, thanks to superb hat-tricks by Jermaine Pennant, who was making his first Premiership start, and Robert Pires.

With both clubs resting a host of first-team regulars, the game was hardly a meaningful Millennium dress-rehearsal, but at least Arsenal spirits were restored by an exhilaratingly fluent performance.

Oddly enough in view of the rout which followed, it was the Saints who threatened first when Tessem burst between Luzhny and Stepanovs, but he was foiled by the alert Taylor and Fernandes blazed high from the rebound.

The hosts' retaliation could hardly have been more crushing. First Kanu combined neatly with skipper-for-the-night Parlour, whose shot was repelled by Jones only for Pires to smack the loose ball into the roof of the net from a narrow angle.

Next Kanu, Henry and van Bronckhorst set up Pennant to score with a lovely low

1 SOUTHAMPTON

Tessem 34

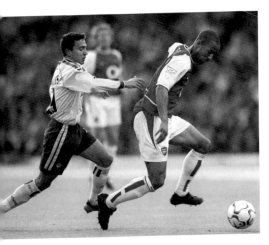

Left *Debutant Ryan Garry marked his first Premiership start with a mature and composed performance.*

Below, right *Jermaine Pennant is unable to contain his delight at becoming the first Gunner since Ian Wright to score a hat-trick on his full League debut.*

shot and then, after Jones had saved from Henry, the 20-year-old Midlander nodded his second and Arsenal's third.

With Gordon Strachan's men in utter disarray, Henry sent in Pires to register with a crisp near-post drive, and Pennant became the first Gunner since Ian Wright to deliver three goals on his full League debut when he raced on to a clever pass from Henry to fire beyond the shell-shocked Jones.

At five down, the visitors rallied slightly when Tessem beat Stepanovs to a cross from Bridge and turned the ball past Taylor, but shortly after the interval Arsenal took charge once more.

Telfer stumbled while attempting to clear and conceded possession to Pires, who contributed the most memorable goal of the night with a beautiful chip which cleared Jones from 30 yards.

Thereafter, with the Gunners cruising, Southampton strove for respectability, but Michael Svensson missed one inviting chance, Beattie failed twice when well placed and young Garry made a timely goal-line clearance.

BOOKINGS

Arsenal Henry 72
Southampton A Svensson 4

FA Barclaycard Premiership
Sunday 11 May 2003 at the Stadium of Light, 3.00 p.m.

SUNDERLAND 0

1	Thomas SORENSEN
18	Darren WILLIAMS
17	Jody CRADDOCK
12	Joachim BJORKLUND
3	Michael GRAY
29	Chris BLACK
8	Gavin McCANN
24	Sean THORNTON
11	Kevin KILBANE
19	Kevin KYLE
10	Kevin PHILLIPS

Substitutes

40	Mart POOM
27	George McCARTNEY (Williams) 46
28	John OSTER (Black) 46
36	Richie RYAN (Thornton) 46
32	Michael PROCTOR

MATCH REPORT

Arsenal cantered to a comfortable victory against the bottom-of-the-table Wearsiders, who were powerless to prevent a 15th successive defeat.

The result, which might have been even more emphatic had the Gunners' finishing matched their approach play, began when Thornton conceded possession to Bergkamp, who slipped a neat pass to Henry. The Frenchman, demonstrating the sublime quality which earned him both footballer of the year awards, netted with a precisely angled shot.

Soon Sunderland were cut open again when Pires' lofted pass landed at the feet of Henry on the left and his flicked cross put in Bergkamp, who drove fiercely against an upright from six yards.

As the siege continued, Sorensen pulled off a memorable parry from a savage Henry half-volley, and the follow-up was blocked too.

The home defence had no answer, however, when Bergkamp delivered from the right to Henry, who nodded into the path of Ljungberg, enabling the Swede to control neatly before volleying home from six yards.

Thierry Henry bursts through a crowd of Sunderland defenders en route to goal.

The second period brought no respite for Mick McCarthy's men, and the overworked Sorensen had already plunged to his left to repel a cross-shot from Henry when the same player rolled an elegant pass between two defenders to find Ljungberg unmarked with the goal at his mercy. He stopped dead, measured his chip from eight yards and Arsenal were three in front.

All that remained was for the Gunners to celebrate their third hat-trick in the space of

4 ARSENAL

Henry 7, Ljungberg 39, 77, 88

1	David SEAMAN
28	Kolo TOURE
22	Oleg LUZHNY
26	Igors STEPANOVS
3	Ashley COLE
8	Fredrik LJUNGBERG
19	GILBERTO Silva
15	Ray PARLOUR
7	Robert PIRES
10	Dennis BERGKAMP
14	Thierry HENRY

Substitutes

20	Guillaume WARMUZ
40	Ryan GARRY
16	Giovanni VAN BRONCKHORST (Parlour) 46
21	Jermaine PENNANT (Pires) 63
25	Nwankwo KANU (Bergkamp) 74

Freddie Ljungberg dinks the ball over Thomas Sorensen to register his second goal of the game.

five days when Pennant found Henry, who touched on to Ljungberg. This time Freddie danced past two challenges before rolling his close-range effort inside a post in clinical style.

With the FA Cup Final looming, there was worry for Arsène Wenger in the shape of injuries to Parlour and Luzhny, though the Highbury boss could not have been more satisfied with his team's imperious form. Though the Premiership crown had slipped away, still the future looked reassuringly bright.

FA Barclaycard Premiership	11 May 2003						
	P	W	D	L	F	A	Pts
Manchester United	38	25	8	5	74	34	83
ARSENAL	38	23	9	6	85	42	78
Newcastle United	38	21	6	11	63	48	69
Chelsea	38	19	10	9	68	38	67
Liverpool	38	18	10	10	61	41	64
Blackburn Rovers	38	16	12	10	52	43	60
Everton	38	17	8	13	48	49	59
Southampton	38	13	13	12	43	46	52
Manchester City	38	15	6	17	47	54	51
Tottenham Hotspur	38	14	8	16	51	62	50
Middlesbrough	38	13	10	15	48	44	49
Charlton Athletic	38	14	7	17	45	56	49
Birmingham City	38	13	9	16	41	49	48
Fulham	38	13	9	16	41	50	48
Leeds United	38	14	5	19	58	57	47
Aston Villa	38	12	9	17	42	47	45
Bolton Wanderers	38	10	14	14	41	51	44
West Ham United	38	10	12	16	42	59	42
West Bromwich Albion	38	6	8	24	29	65	26
Sunderland	38	4	7	27	21	65	19

BOOKINGS

Sunderland McCann 84

Ljungberg completes his hat-trick with a measured finish.

FA Cup Final
Saturday 17 May at the Millennium Stadium, 3.00 p.m.

ARSENAL 1

Pires 38

1	David SEAMAN
12	LAUREN
5	Martin KEOWN
22	Oleg LUZHNY
3	Ashley COLE
8	Fredrik LJUNGBERG
15	Ray PARLOUR
19	GILBERTO Silva
7	Robert PIRES
10	Dennis BERGKAMP
14	Thierry HENRY

Substitutes

13	Stuart TAYLOR
28	Kolo TOURE
16	Giovanni VAN BRONCKHORST
11	Sylvain WILTORD (Bergkamp) 77
25	Nwankwo KANU

Arsenal, having won the right to wear their traditional red shirts, line-up ahead of the Cup Final.

MATCH REPORT

Arsenal retained the FA Cup through a solitary strike by Robert Pires. Always the dominant force, they fashioned enough scoring opportunities to have prevailed by a far more comfortable margin and finished the season on a high.

For all that, they suffered a couple of late scares, with Seaman saving marvellously from an 83rd-minute Ormerod volley and Cole scrambling a Beattie header off his line in the fifth minute of stoppage time.

The contest began in dramatic fashion with the holders going close to grabbing the earliest goal in FA Cup Final history when Ljungberg's flighted delivery freed Henry on the right, only for Niemi to block the Frenchman's point-blank effort after a mere 30 seconds.

Soon domestic football's man of the season was on the rampage again, cutting past Bridge for another shot which was spilled by Niemi, but the danger was cleared by Baird.

After Niemi had frustrated Henry for a third time, Southampton created their first meaningful opening and they wasted it, the unmarked Michael Svensson volleying high from 12 yards following a long throw.

But just as the Saints' confidence began to grow, Arsenal took the lead when a Bergkamp pass from the right squirted away from Ljungberg and fell to Pires, who beat Niemi with a crisply struck drive from eight yards.

Shortly after the break Ljungberg seemed certain to register in his third succes-

0 SOUTHAMPTON

14	**Antti NIEMI**
32	**Chris BAIRD**
5	**Claus LUNDEKVAM**
11	**Michael SVENSSON**
3	**Wayne BRIDGE**
33	**Paul TELFER**
8	**Matt OAKLEY**
12	**Anders SVENSSON**
4	**Chris MARSDEN**
36	**Brett ORMEROD**
9	**James BEATTIE**

Substitutes

1	**Paul JONES (Niemi) 66**
6	**Paul WILLIAMS**
20	**Danny HIGGINBOTHAM**
29	**Fabrice FERNANDES (Baird) 86**
21	**Jo TESSEM (A Svensson) 75**

Stand-in skipper David Seaman lifts the Cup with club captain Patrick Vieira, who had been ruled out of the Final through injury.

BOOKINGS

Arsenal Keown 29, Henry 68
Southampton Beattie 31, Telfer 60, Marsden 76, M Svensson 90

sive final when Niemi parried a Bergkamp curler, but the Swede's shot hit the side-netting.

As Southampton struggled for parity, Telfer nodded high from an Oakley corner before the Gunners returned immediately to the offensive when Henry wriggled through to demand a fingertip save from Niemi.

Thereafter, though Gordon Strachan's men fought gallantly, they didn't threaten seriously until Ormerod's testing of Seaman and Cole's last-ditch heroics. As for the inspired Henry, he deserved a goal but he was denied by substitute 'keeper Jones, and the game finished to a rousing chorus of '1-0 to the Arsenal'.

Robert Pires fires home the game's only goal as Saints' Michael Svensson arrives too late to block.

FA BARCLAYCARD PREMIERSHIP

Sun Aug 18	Birmingham City (H)	2-0	3
Sat Aug 24	West Ham United (A)	2-2	4
Tue Aug 27	West Bromwich Albion (H)	5-1	1
Sun Sep 1	Chelsea (A)	1-1	2
Tue Sep 10	Manchester City (H)	2-1	1
Sat Sep 14	Charlton Athletic (A)	3-0	1
Sat Sep 21	Bolton Wanderers (H)	2-1	1
Sat Sep 28	Leeds United (A)	4-1	1
Sun Oct 6	Sunderland (H)	3-1	1
Sat Oct 19	Everton (A)	1-2	2
Sat Oct 26	Blackburn Rovers (H)	1-2	2
Sun Nov 3	Fulham (A)	1-0	2
Sat Nov 9	Newcastle United (H)	1-0	2
Sat Nov 16	Tottenham Hotspur (H)	3-0	1
Sat Nov 23	Southampton (A)	2-3	1
Sat Nov 30	Aston Villa (H)	3-1	1
Sat Dec 7	Manchester United	0-2	1
Sun Dec 15	Tottenham Hotspur (A)	1-1	1
Sat Dec 21	Middlesbrough (H)	2-0	1
Thu Dec 26	West Bromwich Albion	2-1	1
Sun Dec 29	Liverpool (H)	1-1	1
Wed Jan 1	Chelsea (H)	3-2	1
Sun Jan 12	Birmingham City (A)	4-0	1
Sun Jan 19	West Ham United (H)	3-1	1
Wed Jan 29	Liverpool (A)	2-2	1
Sat Feb 1	Fulham (H)	2-1	1
Sun Feb 9	Newcastle United (A)	1-1	1
Sat Feb 22	Manchester City (A)	5-1	1
Sun Mar 2	Charlton Athletic (H)	2-0	1
Sat Mar 15	Blackburn Rovers (A)	0-2	1
Sun Mar 23	Everton (H)	2-1	1
Sat Apr 5	Aston Villa (A)	1-1	1
Wed Apr 16	Manchester United (H)	2-2	2
Sat Apr 19	Middlesbrough (A)	2-0	2
Sat Apr 26	Bolton Wanderers (A)	2-2	2
Sun May 4	Leeds United (H)	2-3	2
Wed May 7	Southampton (H)	6-1	2
Sun May 11	Sunderland (A)	4-0	2

FA CUP SPONSORED BY AXA

Sat Jan 4	Oxford United (H)	2-0	
Sat Jan 25	Farnborough Town (A*)	5-1	
Sat Feb 15	Manchester United (A)	2-0	
Sat Mar 8	Chelsea (H)	2-2	
Tue Mar 25	Chelsea (A)	3-1	
Sun Apr 13	Sheffield United (N+)	1-0	
Sat May 17	FA Cup Final (N~)	1-0	

* played at Highbury

+ played at Old Trafford

~ played at Millennium Stadium

UEFA CHAMPIONS LEAGUE

Tue Sep 17	Borussia Dortmund (H)	2-0	
Wed Sep 25	PSV Eindhoven (A)	4-0	
Wed Oct 2	Auxerre (A)	1-0	
Tue Oct 22	Auxerre (H)	1-2	
Wed Oct 30	Borussia Dortmund (A)	1-2	
Tue Nov 12	PSV Eindhoven (H)	0-0	
Wed Nov 27	Roma (A)	3-1	
Tue Dec 10	Valencia (H)	0-0	
Tue Feb 18	Ajax (H)	1-1	
Wed Feb 26	Ajax (A)	0-0	
Tue Mar 11	Roma (A)	1-1	
Wed Mar 19	Valencia (A)	1-2	

FA COMMUNITY SHIELD

Sat Aug 11	Liverpool (N*)	2-0	

*played at Millennium Stadium

WORTHINGTON CUP

Wed Nov 6	Sunderland (H)	2-3	

	Premiership
	FA Cup
	Worthington Cup
	UEFA Champions League
	Community Sheild
	Total

APPEARANCES (SUBS IN BRACKETS) AND GOALS

T HENRY	37 (0) 24	2 (3) 1	– – –	12 (0) 7	1 (0) 0	52 (3) 32
S CAMPBELL	33 (0) 2	5 (0) 1	– – –	10 (0) 0	1 (0) 0	49 (0) 3
GILBERTO SILVA	32 (3) 0	1 (2) 0	– – –	11 (1) 2	0 (1) 1	44 (7) 3
D SEAMAN	28 (0) 0	5 (0) 0	– – –	9 (0) 0	1 (0) 0	43 (0) 0
A COLE	30 (1) 1	3 (0) 0	– – –	9 (0) 0	1 (0) 0	43 (1) 1
P VIEIRA	24 (0) 3	5 (0) 0	– – –	12 (0) 1	1 (0) 0	42 (0) 4
LAUREN	26 (1) 1	6 (0) 2	– – –	9 (1) 0	1 (0) 0	42 (2) 3
S WILTORD	27 (7) 10	3 (4) 2	– – –	10 (2) 1	1 (0) 0	41 (13) 13
R PIRES	21 (5) 14	5 (1) 1	1 (0) 1	8 (1) 0	– – –	35 (7) 16
M KEOWN	22 (2) 0	5 (0) 0	– – –	4 (1) 0	1 (0) 0	32 (3) 0
D BERGKAMP	23 (6) 4	2 (2) 2	– – –	6 (1) 1	1 (0) 0	32 (9) 7
F LJUNGBERG	19 (1) 6	3 (1) 1	– – –	7 (1) 2	– – –	29 (3) 9
P CYGAN	16 (2) 1	2 (0) 0	– – –	9 (2) 0	– – –	27 (4) 1
R PARLOUR	14 (5) 0	6 (0) 0	– – –	0 (2) 0	1 (0) 0	21 (7) 0
EDU	12 (6) 2	5 (1) 1	– – –	1 (3) 0	1 (0) 0	19 (10) 3
O LUZHNY	11 (6) 0	2 (0) 0	1 (0) 0	3 (1) 0	– – –	17 (7) 0
K TOURE	9 (17) 2	3 (2) 0	1 (0) 0	3 (4) 0	0 (1) 0	16 (24) 2
G VAN BRONCKHORST	9 (11) 1	3 (2) 0	1 (0) 0	2 (2) 0	– – –	15 (15) 1
N KANU	9 (7) 5	1 (0) 0	1 (0) 0	2 (6) 1	– – –	13 (13) 6
S TAYLOR	7 (1) 0	2 (0) 0	1 (0) 0	1 (1) 0	– – –	11 (2) 0
F JEFFERS	2 (14) 2	6 (0) 3	1 (0) 1	1 (4) 0	– – –	10 (18) 6
R SHAABAN	3 (0) 0	– – –	– – –	2 (0) 0	– – –	5 (0) 0
I STEPANOVS	2 (0) 0	– – –	1 (0) 0	1 (0) 0	– – –	4 (0) 0
J PENNANT	1 (4) 3	– – –	1 (0) 0	0 (1) 0	– – –	2 (5) 3
S SVARD	– – –	1 (0) 0	1 (0) 0	– – –	– – –	2 (0) 0
R GARRY	1 (0) 0	– – –	0 (1) 0	– – –	– – –	1 (1) 0
S TAVLARIDIS	0 (1) 0	– – –	1 (0) 0	– – –	– – –	1 (1) 0
M UPSON	– – –	1 (0) 0	– – –	– – –	– – –	1 (0) 0
J ALIADIERE	0 (3) 1	– – –	– – –	– – –	– – –	0 (3) 1
D BENTLEY	– – –	0 (1) 0	– – –	– – –	– – –	0 (1) 0
M VOLZ	– – –	– – –	0 (1) 0	– – –	– – –	0 (1) 0
J HOYTE	0 (1) 0	– – –	– – –	– – –	– – –	0 (1) 0

JEREMIE ALIADIERE

Position forward
Squad number 30
Born Rambouillet, France, 30 March 1983
Joined Arsenal as scholar in summer 1999, professional in March 2000
Senior Arsenal debut 27 November 2001 v Grimsby Town at Highbury
(League Cup, as substitute)
Arsenal record League: 0 (4) games, 1 goal; League Cup: 0 (2) games,
0 goals; Total: 0 (6) games, 1 goal

In 2002-03 Jeremie enhanced his status as a glittering prospect when called up for Premiership duty in August, looking comfortable at that level and scoring against West Bromwich Albion. The impetus of the pacy, stylish French under-21 international was interrupted by a mid-term hernia, but his sharp springtime form for the reserves emphasised that it was only a temporary setback.

DAVID BENTLEY

Position forward
Squad number 35
Born Peterborough, 27 August 1984
Joined Arsenal as scholar in summer 2000, professional in December 2001
Senior Arsenal debut 4 January 2003 v Oxford United at Highbury
(FA Cup, as substitute)
Arsenal record FA Cup 0 (1) game, 0 goals; Total: 0 (1) game, 0 goals

In 2002-03 David broke into the senior ranks with a 15-minute FA Cup cameo against Oxford in which he showed unmistakable signs of class. Hailed as one of the premier talents of his generation, the England under-19s captain contributed a selection of sumptuous goals for the reserves, revealing touch and vision reminiscent of a young Bergkamp. Watch this space.

DENNIS BERGKAMP

Position forward
Squad number 10
Born Amsterdam, 10 May 1969
Other clubs Ajax, Internazionale
Joined Arsenal from Internazionale in July 1995
Senior Arsenal debut 20 August 1995 v Middlesbrough at Highbury (League)
Arsenal honours League Championship 1997-98, 2001-02; FA Cup 2001-02, 2002-03

Arsenal record League: 204 (30) games, 73 goals; FA Cup: 26 (5) games, 13 goals; League Cup: 15 games, 8 goals; Europe: 28 (6) games, 10 goals; Charity/Community Shield: 2 games, 0 goals; Total: 275 (41) games, 104 goals
Holland caps: 79
In 2002-03 Dennis continued to demonstrate his quality with a series of high-class displays, completing his century of goals for the Gunners in the process. Though not as prolific a scorer as in previous campaigns, the Dutchman excelled as a creator of chances for the likes of Henry and Pires, the stealth, accuracy and imagination of his passing a joy to behold.

SOL CAMPBELL

Position defender
Squad number 23
Born Newham, London, 18 September 1974
Other club Tottenham Hotspur
Joined Arsenal from Tottenham Hotspur in July 2001
Senior Arsenal debut 18 August 2001 v Middlesbrough at The Riverside (League)
Arsenal honours League Championship 2001-02; FA Cup 2001-02
Arsenal record League: 62 (2) games, 4 goals; FA Cup: 12 games, 2 goals; Europe: 20 games, 0 goals; Community Shield: 1 game, 0 goals; Total: 95 (2) games, 6 goals
England caps 53
In 2002-03 Sol went from strength to strength, emerging as the cornerstone of an Arsenal rearguard which lacked continuity due to a plague of injuries. With his speed off the mark and prodigious strength, there was no more effective protector of the ball in the Premiership.

ASHLEY COLE

Position defender
Squad number 3
Born Stepney, London, 20 December 1980
Other club Crystal Palace on loan
Joined Arsenal as trainee in summer 1997, professional in November 1998
Senior Arsenal debut 30 November 1999 v Middlesbrough at The Riverside (League Cup, as substitute)
Arsenal honours League Championship 2001-02; FA Cup 2001-02, 2002-03

Arsenal record League: 75 (3) games, 6 goals; FA Cup: 12 (1) games, 0 goals; League Cup: 1 (1) games, 0 goals; Europe: 23 (2) games, 0 goals; Community Shield: 1 game, 0 goals; Total: 112 (7) games, 6 goals
England caps 17

In 2002-03 Ashley confirmed his status as England's top left-back, continuing to dazzle as an attacker while honing the all-important defensive side of his game, revealing new depths of maturity and reliability. Sadly the speedy Londoner was sidelined in the spring by a hernia operation, but returned in time to play a telling part in the battle for League and FA Cup honours.

PASCAL CYGAN

Position central defender
Squad number 18
Born Lens, France, 29 April 1974
Other clubs Valenciennes, ES Wasquehal, Lille
Joined Arsenal from Lille in July 2002
Senior Arsenal debut 1 September 2002 v Chelsea at Stamford Bridge (League, as substitute)
Arsenal record League: 16 (2) games, 1 goal; FA Cup: 2 games, 0 goals; Europe: 9 (2) games, 0 goals; Total: 27 (4) games, 1 goal

In 2002-03 Pascal made an impressive start, slotting in smoothly alongside Campbell when Keown was injured in the autumn. He proved strong in the air, a robust tackler and an accurate passer with his left foot. The Frenchman grew in confidence throughout the season and notched his first goal with a header at home to Everton in March.

EDU

Position midfielder
Squad number 17
Born Sao Paulo, Brazil, 16 May 1978
Other clubs Sao Paulo, Corinthians
Joined Arsenal from Corinthians in January 2001
Senior Arsenal debut 20 January 2001 v Leicester City at Filbert Street (League, as substitute)
Arsenal honours League Championship 2001-02; FA Cup 2001-02
Arsenal record League: 22 (15) games, 3 goals; FA Cup: 9 (2) games, 2 goals; League Cup: 3 games, 1 goal; Europe: 3 (6) games, 0 goals; Community Shield: 1 game, 0 goals; Total: 38 (23) games, 6 goals

In 2002-03 Edu blossomed into a high-quality and trusted member of the squad, having settled in England and added self-belief to his undoubted technical gifts. Frequently the Brazilian excelled as an ideal attacking foil for Vieira or Gilberto in central midfield, his penetrative passing and his tackling crisp, and it was a pity that his momentum was interrupted by niggling injuries.

RYAN GARRY

Position defender
Squad number 40
Born Hornchurch, 29 September 1983
Joined Arsenal as scholar in summer 2000, professional in summer 2001
Senior Arsenal debut 6 November 2002 v Sunderland at Highbury (Worthington Cup, as substitute)
Arsenal record League: 1 game, 0 goals; League Cup: 0 (1) game, 0 goals; Total: 1 (1) games, 0 goals

In 2002-03 Ryan stepped fleetingly into the senior limelight, doing enough to demonstrate his poise, athleticism and versatility. By choice a central defender, the England under-19 international looked assured at left-back against Southampton, and on the left of midfield against Sunderland. He was effective, too, when facing Chelsea reserves as a striker. An intriguing future awaits.

GILBERTO

Position midfielder
Squad number 19
Born Lagoa da Prata, Brazil, 7 October 1976
Other clubs America MG, Atletico Mineiro
Joined Arsenal from Atletico Mineiro in July 2002
Senior Arsenal debut 11 August 2002 at Millennium Stadium v Liverpool (Community Shield, as substitute)
Arsenal honours FA Cup 2002-03
Arsenal record League: 32 (3) games, 0 goals; FA Cup: 1 (2) games, 0 goals; Europe: 11 (1) games, 2 goals; Community Shield: 0 (1) game, 1 goal; Total: 44 (7) games, 3 goals
Brazil caps 19
In 2002-03 As might be expected of a man who had just pocketed a World Cup winner's medal, Gilberto completed a supremely effective first season as a Gunner. A prodigious ground-coverer in front of the back four, the Brazilian broke up countless attacks and freed Vieira to surge forward. Organised and disciplined, brimming with energy and desire, he proved a dynamic addition to Arsène Wenger's team.

THIERRY HENRY

Position forward
Squad number 14
Born Paris, 17 August 1977
Other clubs AS Monaco, Juventus
Joined Arsenal from Juventus in August 1999
Senior Arsenal debut 7 August 1999 v Leicester City at Highbury (League, as substitute)
Arsenal honours League Championship 2001-02; FA Cup 2001-02, 2002-03
Arsenal record League: 121 (15) games, 82 goals; FA Cup: 12 (5) games, 3 goals; League Cup: 2 games, 1 goal; Europe: 44 (5) games, 26 goals; Community Shield: 1 game, 0 goals; Total: 180 (25) games, 112 goals
France caps 46
In 2002-03 Thierry established compelling credentials as tone of the most thrilling footballers in the world, yet Arsène Wenger is convinced that the best of the double Footballer of the Year is yet to come! He scored goals almost at will, created even more for his colleagues and delighted everyone who prizes the remarkable in sport by his searing runs, fabulous balance, impudent control and frequently exquisite finishing.

CRAIG HOLLOWAY
Position goalkeeper
Squad number 41
Born Blackheath, 10 August 1984
Joined Arsenal as scholar in summer 2000, professional in 2002
In 2002-03 Craig's career took a major move into the ascendant when he was promoted to the first team squad in 2002.
The Londoner, who signed his first professional contract with Arsenal in the summer of 2000, played eight times for the reserves, having played 23 under-19s games in 2001-02, including both legs of the successful play-off final against Liverpool.

JUSTIN HOYTE
Position defender
Squad number 42
Born Waltham Forest, 20 November 1984
Joined Arsenal as scholar in summer 2001, as professional in July 2002
Senior Arsenal debut 7 May 2003 v Southampton at Highbury (League, as substitute)
Arsenal record League: 0 (1) games, 0 goals; Total: 0 (1) games, 0 goals

In 2002-03 Justin entered the senior reckoning for the first time, albeit only as a late substitute for Jermaine Pennant at home to Southampton in the spring. A cool, skilful operator who has excelled in the junior ranks both at right-back and in central defence, he is a magnificent all-round athlete and a particularly gifted sprinter who has featured regularly for England under-19s.

FRANCIS JEFFERS

Position forward
Squad number 9
Born Liverpool, 25 January 1981
Other club Everton
Joined Arsenal from Everton in June 2001
Senior Arsenal debut 21 August 2001 v Leeds United at Highbury
(League, as substitute)
Arsenal record League: 4 (18) games, 4 goals; FA Cup: 7 (1) games,
3 goals; Europe: 1 (6) games, 0 goals; Total: 13 (25) games, 8 goals
England caps 1
In 2002-03 In a footballing sense, Francis came of age. Having shrugged off the long-term injury jinx which had dogged him both at Everton and in his first season as a Gunner, he showed himself to be a goalscorer of immense potential. Though his Premiership starts were few, he contributed crucial strikes as his confidence burgeoned, and garnered further reward with a goal on his full England debut against Australia.

NWANKWO KANU

Position forward
Squad number 25
Born Owerri, Nigeria, 1 August 1976
Other clubs Federation Works, Iwuanyanwu, Ajax, Internazionale
Joined Arsenal from Internazionale in January 1999
Senior Arsenal debut 13 February 1999 v Sheffield United at Highbury
(FA Cup, as substitute, match void)
Arsenal honours League Championship 2001-02; FA Cup 2001-02
Arsenal record League: 60 (49) games, 29 goals; FA Cup: 4 (10)
games, 3 goals; League Cup: 4 games, 2 goals; Europe: 26 (20) games, 6 goals; Charity Shield:
1 game, 1 goal; Total: 95 (79) games, 41 goals
Nigeria caps 36
In 2002-03 Kanu came close to his beguiling best during an autumn purple patch in which he scored six goals in seven senior outings, and the giant Nigerian seemed set fair for a productive season. But then he fell prey to a succession of niggling injuries and, with Jeffers making huge advances, he found himself on the sidelines too frequently for his liking. Still, though, he offered a potent attacking option.

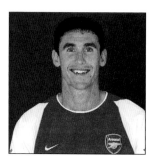

MARTIN KEOWN
Position defender
Squad number 5
Born Oxford, 24 July 1966
Other clubs Brighton on loan, Aston Villa, Everton
Joined Arsenal as trainee in June 1982, as professional in February 1984, from Everton in February 1993
Senior Arsenal debut 23 November 1985 v West Bromwich Albion at The Hawthorns (League)
Arsenal honours League Championship 1997-98, 2001-02; FA Cup 1997-98, 2001-02, 2002-03
Arsenal record League: 301 (21) games, 4 goals; FA Cup: 36 (3) games, 0 goals; League Cup: 18 (2) games, 1 goal; Europe: 42 (7) games, 3 goals; Charity/Community Shield: 3 (1) games, 0 goals; Total: 400 (34) games, 8 goals
England caps 43
In 2002-03 Martin remained the epitome of iron-willed aggression at the core of the Gunners' rearguard. When he was replaced by Cygan because of injury in September, it seemed possible that the 36-year-old warrior might be forced to step aside. But back he bounced, still eager for the fray, and he ended the season with a faultless display against Southampton in the Cup Final.

LAUREN
Position defender or midfielder
Squad number 12
Born Londi Kribi, Cameroon, 19 January 1977
Other clubs Utrera, Seville, Levante, Real Mallorca
Joined Arsenal from Real Mallorca in May 2000
Senior Arsenal debut 19 August 2000 v Sunderland at the Stadium of Light (League, as substitute)
Arsenal honours League Championship 2001-02; FA Cup 2001-02, 2002-03
Arsenal record League: 68 (4) games, 5 goals; FA Cup: 13 games, 2 goals; Europe: 26 (6) games, 1 goal; Community Shield: 1 game, 0 goals; Total: 108 (10) games, 8 goals
Cameroon caps 22
In 2002-03 Lauren attained new levels of consistent excellence at right-back, whether slaloming down the touchline in all-out attack or defending soundly and sensibly. The skilful Cameroonian, who announced his retirement from international football at the age of 25, returned to top form after a mid-season ankle injury.

FREDRIK LJUNGBERG
Position midfielder
Squad number 8
Born Halmstads, Sweden, 16 April 1977
Other club Halmstads
Joined Arsenal from Halmstads in September 1998
Senior Arsenal debut 20 September 1998 v Manchester United at Highbury (League, as substitute)
Arsenal honours League Championship 2001-02; FA Cup 2001-02, 2002-03

Arsenal record League: 100 (17) games, 31 goals; FA Cup: 16 (3) games, 4 goals; League Cup: 2 games, 0 goals; Europe: 36 (8) games, 9 goals; Charity Shield: 1 game, 0 goals; Total: 155 (28) games, 44 goals
Sweden caps 36
In 2002-03 Though Freddie's season was scarred by injury – he missed the first month with hip damage and 14 games after Christmas with an Achilles problem – still he made a sizeable contribution to the quest for honours. When fully fit the multi-talented Swede was as elusive as ever, with his characteristic late runs into the box, and was equally impressive on either midfield flank

OLEG LUZHNY
Position defender
Squad number 22
Born Kiev, Ukraine, 5 August 1968
Other clubs Volyn Lutsk, Karpaty Lvov, Dynamo Kiev
Joined Arsenal from Dynamo Kiev in June 1999
Senior Arsenal debut 1 August 1999 v Manchester United at Wembley (Charity Shield, as substitute)
Arsenal honours League Championship 2001-02; FA Cup 2002-03
Arsenal record League: 58 (17) games, 0 goals; FA Cup: 9 games, 0 goals; League Cup: 4 games, 0 goals; Europe: 20 (1) games, 0 goals; Charity Shield: 0 (1) game, 0 goals; Total: 91 (19) games, 0 goals
Ukraine caps 38
USSR caps 15
In 2002-03 Oleg proved an admirable deputy right-back when Lauren was sidelined in November, showing the Highbury faithful precisely why he was nicknamed 'The Galloping Horse' during his Dynamo Kiev years. His strength and stamina were supplemented by flashes of skill, and it was a shame when the Ukrainian's surge was halted by a calf injury. Oleg also figured as a stand-in centre-half, playing with great composure in that position against Southampton in the Cup Final.

137

RAY PARLOUR
Position midfielder
Squad number 15
Born Romford, 7 March 1973
Joined Arsenal as trainee in summer 1989, professional in March 1991
Senior Arsenal debut 29 January 1992 v Liverpool at Anfield (League)
Arsenal honours League Championship 1997-98, 2001-02; FA Cup 1992-93, 1997-98, 2001-02, 2002-03; League Cup 1992-93
Arsenal record League: 266 (48) games, 22 goals; FA Cup: 38 (3) games, 4 goals; League Cup: 20 (3) games, 0 goals; Europe: 37 (11) games, 5 goals; Charity/Community Shield: 3 games, 1 goal; Total: 364 (65) games, 32 goals
England caps 10
In 2002-03 after suffering the longest lay-off of his career with a hamstring injury, Ray did not recapture a regular place in midfield, though often he played impressively when selected. Yet again he proved himself capable of shining both wide on the right and in a central position, emphasising his quality with a combination of vast experience, endless industry and oft-underrated skill.

JERMAINE PENNANT
Position midfielder
Squad number 21
Born Nottingham, 15 January 1983
Other clubs Notts County, Watford on loan
Joined Arsenal from Notts County as trainee in January 1999
Senior Arsenal debut 30 November 1999 v Middlesbrough at The Riverside (League Cup, as substitute)
Arsenal record League: 1 (4) games, 3 goals; League Cup: 5 (1) games, 0 goals; Europe: 0 (3) games, 0 goals; Total: 6 (8) games, 3 goals
In 2002-03 Jermaine flitted around the fringes of the senior squad, but the plethora of world-class stars made it hard to break through until the injury crisis in the spring. Then he made up for lost time with a beautifully taken hat-trick against Southampton, having earned lavish praise earlier, during a second loan stint at Watford. A richly talented attacking midfielder, his time will surely come.

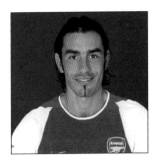

ROBERT PIRES

Position midfielder
Squad number 7
Born Reims, France, 29 January 1973
Other clubs Stade de Reims, FC Metz, Olympique Marseille
Joined Arsenal from Olympique Marseille in July 2000
Senior Arsenal debut 19 August 2000 v Sunderland at the Stadium of Light (League, as substitute)
Arsenal honours League Championship 2001-02; FA Cup 2002-03
Arsenal record League: 77 (10) games, 27 goals; FA Cup: 14 (3) games, 5 goals; League Cup: 1 game, 1 goal; Europe: 31 (2) games, 4 goals; Total: 123 (15) games, 37 goals
France caps 54
In 2002-03 Robert made an astonishingly rapid return to prime form following his serious knee injury. Once more his distribution and dribbling were brilliant, his entire game was infused with imagination, and he weighed in with plenty of important goals, including the winning strike in the Cup Final. Roaming freely from his customary starting position on the left flank, he was the complete play-maker.

DAVID SEAMAN

Position goalkeeper
Squad number 1
Born Rotherham, 19 September 1963
Other clubs Peterborough United, Birmingham City, Queen's Park Rangers
Joined Arsenal from Queen's Park Rangers in May 1990
Senior Arsenal debut 25 August 1990 v Wimbledon at Plough Lane (League)
Arsenal honours European Cup Winners' Cup 1993-94; League Championship 1990-91, 1997-98, 2001-02; FA Cup 1992-93, 1997-98, 2001-02, 2002-03; League Cup 1992-93
Arsenal record League: 405 games, 0 goals; FA Cup: 48 games, 0 goals; League Cup: 38 games, 0 goals; Europe: 69 games, 0 goals; Charity/Community Shield: 4 games, 0 goals; Total: 564 games, 0 goals
England caps 75
In 2002-03 David continued to confound the sceptics who reckoned that nobody in his fortieth year could hold his own in the Premiership. In fact, not only did his hunger for honours remain as sharp as ever as he passed his 1,000th senior game (including internationals) in his 21st season of League football, but his performance level kept pace with it. He ended the season on a high by captaining Arsenal to success in the FA Cup Final.

RAMI SHAABAN
Position goalkeeper
Squad number 24
Born Stockholm, Sweden, 30 June 1975
Other clubs Djurgaardens
Joined Arsenal from Djurgaardens in August 2002
Senior Arsenal debut 12 November 2002 v PSV Eindhoven at Highbury (Champions League)
Arsenal record League: 3 games, 0 goals; Europe: 2 games, 0 goals; Total: 5 games, 0 goals

In 2002-03 Rami made a dream start to his Arsenal career, keeping a clean sheet against PSV Eindhoven and looking agile, alert and reassuringly strong. However, after only a handful of outings, he broke his leg in training on Christmas Eve and his immediate prospects were in ruins, leaving the level-headed Swede to buckle down to a lengthy programme of recuperation.

IGORS STEPANOVS
Position defender
Squad number 26
Born Ogre, Latvia, 21 January 1976
Other club Skonto Riga
Joined Arsenal from Skonto Riga in September 2000
Senior Arsenal debut 1 November 2000 v Ipswich Town at Highbury (League Cup)
Arsenal record League: 17 games, 0 goals; FA Cup: 4 games, 0 goals; League Cup: 4 (1) games, 1 goal; Europe: 4 (1) games, 0 goals; Total: 29 (2) games, 1 goal
Latvia caps 48

In 2002-03 Though unable to claim a first-team berth, Igors was a regular on the Champions League bench and he found an important role as captain of the reserves, his extensive experience proving hugely beneficial to the club's youngsters. On the international front, Igors excelled for Latvia in their Euro 2004 qualifiers.

SEBASTIAN SVARD
Position midfielder
Squad number 31
Born Denmark, 15 January 1983
Other club FC Copenhagen
Joined Arsenal from FC Copenhagen in November 2000
Senior Arsenal debut 27 November 2001 v Grimsby Town at Highbury
(League Cup, as substitute)
Arsenal record FA Cup: 1 game, 0 goals; League Cup: 1 (1) game,
0 goals; Total: 2 (1) games, 0 goals

In 2002-03 After playing much of his early football as a left-back and central defender, Sebastian made substantial strides as a midfield holding player, his physically imposing style based on that of his mentor, Patrick Vieira. The Danish under-21 international took the eye on his cup outings against Sunderland and Oxford, and will be striving for further impact in 2003-04.

STATHIS TAVLARIDIS
Position defender
Squad number 27
Born Greece, 25 January 1980
Other clubs Elpida Provata, Iraklis Saloniki, Portsmouth on loan
Joined Arsenal from Iraklis in September 2001
Senior Arsenal debut 5 November 2001 v Manchester United at
Highbury (League Cup)
Arsenal record League: 0 (1) game, 0 goals; League Cup: 4 games,
0 goals; Total: 4 (1) games, 0 goals

In 2002-03 The Greek under-21 international centre-half was granted only one senior start, against Sunderland in the Worthington Cup, but formed a steady partnership with Stepanovs in the reserves as he sought to settle in the English game. In January Stathis was loaned to Portsmouth, making his debut for the First Division pacesetters in an FA Cup clash with Manchester United.

STUART TAYLOR

Position goalkeeper
Squad number 13
Born Romford, 28 November 1980
Other clubs Bristol Rovers on loan, Crystal Palace on loan, Peterborough United on loan
Senior Arsenal debut 1 November 2000 v Ipswich Town at Highbury (League Cup)
Arsenal honours League Championship 2001-02
Arsenal record League: 16 (2) games, 0 goals; FA Cup: 3 games, 0 goals; League Cup: 4 games, 0 goals; Europe: 3 (2) games, 0 goals; Total: 26 (4) games, 0 goals
In 2002-03 Stuart built solidly on his progress of the previous campaign, reacting positively to the arrivals of Shaaban and Warmuz and giving a succession of superb displays – notably away to Manchester City and at Stamford Bridge in the FA Cup – when deputising for the injured Seaman. Big, brave, athletic and still young for a 'keeper, he is a tremendous long-term prospect.

KOLO TOURE

Position midfielder or defender
Squad number 28
Born Ivory Coast, 19 March 1981
Other club Asec Mimosas
Joined Arsenal from Asec Mimosas in February 2002
Senior Arsenal debut 11 August 2002 v Liverpool at Millennium Stadium (Community Shield, as substitute)
Arsenal record League: 9 (17) games, 2 goals; FA Cup: 3 (2) games, 0 goals; League Cup: 1 game, 0 goals; Europe: 3 (4) games, 0 goals; Community Shield: 0 (1) game, 0 goals; Total: 16 (24) games, 2 goals
Ivory Coast caps 23
In 2002-03 Kolo was a revelation, bringing an appealing cocktail of insatiable zest, grass-burning pace and immense power to a succession of roles. At various times he excelled in both full-back slots, on both flanks of midfield, and in his international position of central defender.

GIOVANNI VAN BRONCKHORST

Position midfielder or defender
Squad number 16
Born Rotterdam, 5 February 1975
Other clubs Feyenoord, Waalwijk on loan, Glasgow Rangers
Joined Arsenal from Glasgow Rangers in June 2001
Senior Arsenal debut 18 August 2001 v Middlesbrough at The Riverside (League, as substitute)
Arsenal record League Championship 2001-02
Arsenal record League: 22 (19) games, 2 goals; FA Cup: 5 (2) games, 0 goals; League Cup: 4 games, 0 goals; Europe: 8 (3) games, 0 goals; Total: 39 (24) games, 2 goals
Holland caps 28

In 2002-03 Giovanni returned to the first-team fold in November following knee damage suffered nine months earlier. After a few games in his premier position of midfielder, the adaptable Dutch international was pressed into a lengthy spell of left-back duty because of injury to Cole. A box-to-box dynamo who passes perceptively and is a dead-ball expert, he is a massive asset to the squad.

PATRICK VIEIRA

Position midfielder
Squad number 4
Born Dakar, Senegal, 23 June 1976
Other clubs Cannes, AC Milan
Joined Arsenal from AC Milan in August 1996
Senior Arsenal debut 16 September 1996 v Sheffield Wednesday at Highbury (League, as substitute)
Arsenal honours: League Championship 1997-98, 2001-02; FA Cup 1997-98, 2001-02
Arsenal record League: 211 (7) games, 19 goals; FA Cup: 35 (2) games, 2 goals; League Cup: 5 games, 0 goals; Europe: 55 games, 2 goals; Charity/Community Shield: 3 games, 0 goals; Total: 309 (9) games, 23 goals
France caps 62

In 2002-03 Relishing the responsibilities of leadership, having succeeded Tony Adams as club captain, Patrick rose to new heights of maturity and performance. He bestrode the centre of midfield like a colossus, his passing and tackling impeccable and his runs from deep virtually unstoppable. Still only 26 but in his seventh season as a Gunner, he has few peers in world football.

143

MORITZ VOLZ
Position midfielder or full-back
Squad number 29
Born Siegen, Germany, 21 January 1983
Other clubs Schalke 04, Wimbledon on loan
Joined Arsenal as scholar in summer 1999, professional in January 2000
Senior Arsenal debut 1 November 2000 v Ipswich Town at Highbury (League Cup)
Arsenal record League Cup: 1 (1) games, 0 goals; Total: 1 (1) games, 0 goals

In 2002-03 Moritz furthered his English footballing education on loan at Wimbledon, putting behind him a demoralising catalogue of injuries, including a broken jaw, which have hindered his impressive development to date. Ceaselessly energetic whether operating at full-back or in midfield, the German under-21 captain loves to get forward but is defensively sound.

GUILLAUME WARMUZ
Position goalkeeper
Squad number 20
Born Saint Vallier, France, France, 22 May 1970
Other clubs Lens
Joined Arsenal on loan from Lens in January 2003
Arsenal record 0 games, 0 goals

In 2002-03 Guillaume was acquired on loan after Shaaban broke his leg in December, and he bedded in with a series of solid displays for the reserves, but was unable to oust Taylor as Seaman's deputy.

Close observers of the Arsenal scene might recall the composed and capable Frenchman facing the Gunners for Lens in a UEFA Cup semi-final at Wembley in the spring of 2000.

SYLVAIN WILTORD
Position forward
Squad number 11
Born Neuilly sur Marne, France, 10 May 1974
Other clubs Rennes, Deportivo La Coruna, Bordeaux
Joined Arsenal from Bordeaux in August 2000
Senior Arsenal debut 6 September 2000 v Chelsea at Highbury
(League, as substitute)
Arsenal honours League Championship 2001-02; FA Cup 2001-02, 2002-03

Arsenal record League: 70 (24) games, 28 goals; FA Cup: 14 (6) games, 10 goals; League Cup: 4 games, 4 goals; Europe: 21 (15) games, 3 goals; Community Shield: 1 game, 0 goals; Total: 110 (45) games, 45 goals
France caps 50
In 2002-03 Sylvain began with a bang, netting six times in six games to top the Premiership goal charts. Thereafter his scoring rate declined, but still there were key strikes to savour, notably the FA Cup clincher against Manchester United at Old Trafford. The Frenchman, operating mainly from the right of midfield, contributed more than goals anyway, working tirelessly and combining sweetly with his fellow attackers.

ARSÈNE WENGER (Manager)
Born Strasbourg, France, 22 October 1949
Clubs as player Mutzig, Mulhouse, Strasbourg
Clubs as manager/coach Strasbourg (youth section), Cannes (assistant), Nancy, AS Monaco, Grampus Eight Nagoya
Honours as manager/coach with AS Monaco - French League Championship 1987-88, French Cup 1990-91, France Manager of the Year 1987-88; with Grampus Eight Nagoya - Emperor's Cup 1996, Japan Super Cup 1996, Japan Manager of the Year 1995; with Arsenal - League Championship 1997-98, 2001-02; FA Cup 1997-98, 2001-02, 2002-03; Manager of the Year 1997-98, 2001-02

Joined Arsenal 1996
In 2002-03 Arsène furnished yet further evidence of his inspirational qualities as a football boss, fielding arguably the most sparklingly attractive side in the club's history. His efforts to retain the Premiership title were frustrated, due partly to a crippling sequence of injuries in the spring, but he regrouped his forces brilliantly and was rewarded with a third FA Cup triumph in the space of six years.

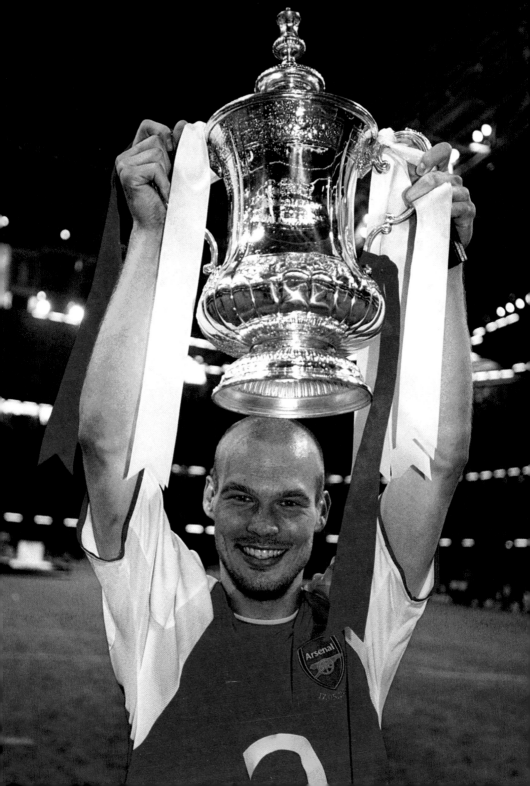

PAT RICE (Assistant Manager)
Born Belfast, 17 March 1949
Clubs as player Arsenal, Watford
Honours as player League Championship 1970-71; FA Cup
1970-71, 1978-79. Won 49 caps for Northern Ireland
Joined Arsenal as coach 1984
Honours as Arsenal coach FA Youth Cup 1987-88, 1993-94; League
Championship 1997-98, 2001-02; FA Cup 1997-98, 2001-02, 2002-03

BORO PRIMARAC (First Team Coach)
Born Mostar, Yugoslavia (now Bosnia), 5 December 1954
Clubs as player Hajduk Split, Cannes, Lille. Captained
Yugoslavia, winning 18 caps
Clubs as coach Cannes, Valenciennes, Grampus Eight Nagoya
Joined Arsenal 1997
Honours as Arsenal coach League Championship 1997-98,
2001-02; FA Cup 1997-98, 2001-02, 2002-03

EDDIE NIEDZWIECKI (Reserve Team Manager)
Born Bangor, Wales, 3 May 1959
Clubs as player Wrexham, Chelsea
Honours as player Division Two Championship with Chelsea
1983-84. Won 2 caps for Wales
Clubs as coach Chelsea, Reading
Joined Arsenal 2000

BOB WILSON (Goalkeeping Coach)
Born Chesterfield, 30 October 1941
Club as player Arsenal
Honours as player European Fairs Cup 1969-70; League
Championship 1970-71; FA Cup 1970-71. Won 2 caps for
Scotland
Joined Arsenal as coach 1976
Retired 2003

GARY LEWIN (Physiotherapist)
Born East Ham, London, 16 May 1964
Clubs as player Arsenal (youth), Barnet
Joined Arsenal as physio 1983
England physio since 1996

COLIN LEWIN (Assistant Physiotherapist)
Born Plaistow, London, 15 September 1973
Joined Arsenal 1995

TONY COLBERT (Fitness Coach)
Born Paddington, London, 29 May 1963
Joined Arsenal 1998

JOEL HARRIS (Chief Masseur)
Born Wimbledon, London, 28 August 1961
Joined Arsenal part-time 1994, full-time 1998

CRAIG GANT (Masseur)

JOHN KELLY (Masseur)

DARREN PAGE (Masseur)

JOHN COOK (Masseur)

STEVE ROWLEY (Chief Scout)
Born Romford, 2 December 1958
Joined Arsenal 1980

VIC AKERS (Kit Manager)
Born Islington, London, 24 August 1946
Clubs as player Slough Town, Cambridge United, Watford
Joined Arsenal as reserve team physio and kit manager 1986
General manager of Arsenal Ladies

PAUL AKERS (Assistant Kit Manager)
Born Bromley, 3 February 1976
Joined Arsenal 2001

PAUL JOHNSON (Equipment Manager)
Born Hackney, 14 March 1961
Joined Arsenal 1981

ALEX BAILEY
Position defender

ADAM BIRCHALL
Position forward

STEPHEN BRADLEY
Position midfielder

JERMAINE BROWN
Position defender

LIAM CHILVERS
Position defender

BEN CHORLEY
Position defender

PATRICK CREGG
Position midfielder

JORDAN FOWLER
Position midfielder

DAVID GRONDIN
Position midfielder

JOHN HALLS
Position defender

INGI HOJSTED
Position midfielder

JUAN
Position defender

SEBASTIAN LARSSON
Position midfielder

NICKY NICOLAU
Position defender

DAVID NOBLE
Position midfielder

STEPHEN O'DONNELL
Position midfielder

PAULINHO
Position midfielder

DEAN SHIELS
Position forward

STEVEN SIDWELL
Position midfielder

FRANKIE SIMEK
Position defender

OLAFUR-INGI SKULASON
Position midfielder

JOHN SPICER
Position midfielder

GRAHAM STACK
Position goalkeeper

JEROME THOMAS
Position midfielder

SECOND YEAR SCHOLARS

BRETT FREEMAN	defender
MICHAEL GORDON	forward
ALFIE KAMARA	defender
SAM KANU	midfielder
WAYNE O'SULLIVAN	midfielder
ASHLEY PROBETS	defender

FIRST YEAR SCHOLARS

MARCUS ARTRY	midfielder
MICHAEL JORDAN	goalkeeper
NEIL KILKENNY	midfielder
DEAN McDONALD	forward
SAM OJI	defender
QUINCEY OWUSU-ABEYIE	forward
DORIAN SMALL	defender
HASSAN SULAIMAN	defender

These players appeared for Arsenal during the 2002-03 season. Some may have since left the Club.

YOUTH DEVELOPMENT STAFF

LIAM BRADY (Head of Youth Development and Academy Director)
Born Dublin, 13 February 1956.
Clubs as player Arsenal, Juventus, Sampdoria, Internazionale, Ascoli, West Ham United.
Honours as player with Arsenal – FA Cup 78/9; with Juventus – Italian Championship 81/2. Won 72 caps for Republic of Ireland
Clubs as coach/manager Celtic, Brighton and Hove Albion
Joined Arsenal coaching staff 1996

DAVID COURT (Assistant Head of Youth Development and Assistant Academy Director)
Born Mitcham, 1 March 1944
Clubs as player Arsenal, Luton Town
Joined Arsenal coaching staff 1996

DON HOWE (Head Youth Coach and Under-19s Coach)
Born Wolverhampton, 12 October 1935
Clubs as player West Bromwich Albion, Arsenal
Honours as player 23 caps for England
Clubs as coach/manager Arsenal (coach), West Bromwich Albion (manager), Leeds United (coach), Galatasaray (coach), Arsenal (coach, then manager), Wimbledon (coach). Also coached for England.
Rejoined Arsenal as coach 1997
Retired 2003

NEIL BANFIELD (Under-17s Coach)
Born Poplar, 20 January 1962
Clubs as player Crystal Palace, Adelaide City, Leyton Orient
Clubs as coach Charlton Athletic
Joined Arsenal 1997

DAVID WALES (Youth Team Physio)
Born Gateshead, 24 August 1972
Joined Arsenal 2001

FA BARCLAYCARD PREMIERSHIP
RESERVE LEAGUE (SOUTH)

Wed Aug 14	Fulham (H)	1-5
Wed Aug 21	West Ham United (A)	2-2
Wed Aug 28	Charlton Athletic (H)	6-1
Wed Sep 18	Watford (A)	4-0
Thu Sep 26	Chelsea (H)	0-2
Mon Sep 30	Wimbledon (A)	4-2
Tue Oct 8	Leicester City (A)	2-0
Wed Oct 23	Ipswich Town (H)	2-0
Wed Oct 30	Nottingham Forest (A)	2-0
Mon Nov 25	Watford (H)	1-1
Wed Dec 11	Coventry City (A)	1-1
Mon Dec 16	Tottenham Hotspur (A)	3-0
Mon Jan 6	Derby County (H)	1-2
Wed Jan 22	Fulham (A)	0-3
Mon Jan 27	Southampton (H)	3-1
Mon Feb 3	Chelsea (A)	1-1
Wed Feb 12	Ipswich Town (A)	0-3
Mon Feb 17	Wimbledon (H)	2-1
Wed Feb 26	Charlton Athletic (A)	1-4
Wed Mar 5	Leicester City (H)	3-3
Wed Mar 12	Nottingham Forest (H)	7-2
Tue Mar 18	Southampton (A)	3-1
Mon Apr 7	Coventry City (H)	4-1
Tues Apr 15	Derby County (A)	0-0
Wed Apr 23	Tottenham Hotspur (H)	2-0
Tues May 6	West Ham United (H)	1-2

APPEARANCES (SUBS IN BRACKETS) AND GOALS

SEBASTIAN SVARD	18	(2)	1
DAVID BENTLEY	17	(2)	7
RYAN GARRY	15	(1)	–
STATHIS TAVLARIDIS	15	(0)	–
JERMAINE BROWN	14	(4)	3
IGORS STEPANOVS	14	(0)	1
JERMAINE PENNANT	13	(0)	9
ALEX BAILEY	13	(4)	–
NICKY NICOLAU	12	(3)	–
JEROME THOMAS	12	(0)	6
JEREMIE ALIADIERE	11	(0)	8
JOHN SPICER	9	(5)	–
MORITZ VOLZ	8	(1)	–
KOLO TOURE	8	(0)	1
GUILLAUME WARMUZ	8	(0)	–
STEVEN SIDWELL	7	(2)	1
JUAN	7	(1)	–
CRAIG HOLLOWAY	7	(1)	–
BEN CHORLEY	7	(0)	–
DAVID GRONDIN	7	(0)	–
STUART TAYLOR	7	(0)	–
JUSTIN HOYTE	6	(4)	–
FRANCIS JEFFERS	6	(0)	8
FRANKIE SIMEK	4	(2)	–
RAMI SHAABAN	4	(0)	–
PAULINHO	3	(5)	1
DAVID NOBLE	3	(2)	1
GRAHAM BARRETT	3	(0)	2
FREDRIK LJUNGBERG	3	(0)	1
PASCAL CYGAN	3	(0)	–
MATTHEW UPSON	3	(0)	–
JORDAN FOWLER	3	(0)	–
OLEG LUZHNY	3	(0)	–
STEPHEN BRADLEY	2	(9)	–
EDU	2	(0)	1
GIO VAN BRONCKHORST	2	(0)	–
SEBASTIAN LARSSON	1	(5)	–
OLAFUR-INGI SKULASON	1	(4)	1
NWANKWO KANU	1	(0)	1
ROBERT PIRES	1	(0)	1
MARTIN KEOWN	1	(0)	–
ASHLEY COLE	1	(0)	–
WAYNE O'SULLIVAN	1	(0)	–
DEAN SHIELS	–	(2)	–
QUINCEY OWUSU-ABEYIE	–	(1)	–
ASHLEY PROBETS	–	(1)	–
Own goals	–	(0)	2

FA Barclaycard Premiership

	P	W	D	L	F	A	Pts
Watford	26	15	5	6	34	27	50
Fulham	26	14	6	6	58	34	48
Derby County	26	13	7	6	46	30	46
ARSENAL	26	13	6	7	56	38	45
West Ham United	26	10	11	5	29	26	41
Tottenham Hotspur	26	10	5	11	32	33	35
Charlton Athletic	26	10	4	12	40	37	34
Nottingham Forest	26	10	4	12	39	42	34
Leicester City	26	10	3	13	31	43	33
Chelsea	26	8	8	10	31	33	32
Ipswich Town	26	9	5	12	34	39	32
Southampton	26	9	5	12	27	38	32
Wimbledon	26	5	6	15	27	44	21
Coventry City	26	4	9	13	18	38	21

FA ACADEMY LEAGUE UNDER-19, GROUP D

Sat Aug 24	Barnsley (A)	1-2	Sat Dec 7	Charlton Athletic (H)	1-0
Sat Aug 31	Sunderland (H)	4-1	Sat Dec 14	Watford (A)	0-3
Sat Sep 7	Chelsea (A)	3-1	Sat Jan 11	Norwich City (H)	0-2
Sat Sep 14	Crystal Palace (H)	4-1	Sat Jan 18	Leicester City (A)	2-0
Sat Sep 21	Millwall (H)	2-2	Sat Jan 25	Tottenham Hotspur (H)	1-0
Sat Sep 28	West Ham United (H)	0-1	Sat Feb 8	Fulham (A)	0-1
Sat Oct 5	Reading (A)	4-1	Sat Feb 15	Southampton	2-0
Sat Oct 12	Ipswich Town (H)	2-0	Sat Feb 22	Bristol City (A)	3-1
Sat Oct 19	Aston Villa (A)	3-3	Sat Mar 1	Coventry City (A)	5-1
Sat Oct 26	Watford (H)	2-0	Sat Mar 8	Wimbledon (H)	2-1
Sat Nov 2	Norwich City (A)	0-0	Sat Mar 15	Charlton Athletic (A)	2-1
Sat Nov 9	Leicester City (H)	3-0	Sat Mar 22	Reading (H)	0-0
Sat Nov 16	Tottenham Hotspur (A)	3-2	Sat Mar 29	Ipswich Town (A)	0-3
Sat Nov 23	Wimbledon (A)	3-2	Sat Apr 5	Aston Villa (H)	1-2

FA League Under 19, Group D

	P	W	D	L	F	A	Pts
Aston Villa	28	18	5	5	71	38	59
ARSENAL	28	17	4	7	53	31	55

FA ACADEMY LEAGUE UNDER-17, GROUP D

Tue Aug 27	Charlton Athletic (H)	5-0	Sat Nov 23	Aston Villa (H)	1-3
Sat Aug 31	Sunderland (H)	4-0	Sat Dec 7	Charlton Athletic (A)	3-4
Sat Sep 7	Fulham (A)	1-2	Sat Dec 14	Watford (H)	2-1
Sat Sep 14	Bolton Wanderers (H)	3-1	Sat Jan 11	Ipswich Town (A)	1-2
Sat Sep 21	Aston Villa (A)	3-4	Sat Jan 18	Leicester City (A)	1-2
Sat Oct 5	Wimbledon (H)	2-0	Sat Jan 25	Tottenham Hotspur (A)	1-3
Sat Oct 12	Southampton (A)	1-1	Sat Feb 8	Wimbledon (A)	5-1
Sat Oct 19	Millwall (H)	2-0	Sat Feb 15	Bristol City (H)	3-0
Sat Oct 26	Watford (A)	1-2	Sat Feb 22	Reading (A)	2-1
Sat Nov 2	Ipswich Town (H)	4-2	Sat Mar 1	Coventry City (H)	5-1
Sat Nov 16	Tottenham Hotspur (H)	2-1	Sat Mar 8	West Ham United (A)	1-1

FA League Under 17, Group D

	P	W	D	L	F	A	Pts
Aston Villa	22	13	8	1	55	30	47
ARSENAL	22	12	2	8	53	32	38

FA League Under 17, Play-offs, Group 5

	P	W	D	L	F	A	Pts
ARSENAL	3	2	0	1	10	3	6
Wolverhampton Wanderers	3	2	0	1	7	9	6

FA ACADEMY LEAGUE UNDER-17, GROUP D

PLAY-OFFS (GROUP 5)

Sat Mar 22	Sheffield Wednesday (H)	0-2
Sat Apr 5	Bristol City (A)	3-0
Sat Apr 26	Wolves (H)	7-1

KNOCK-OUT PHASE

Sat May 3	Coventry City (A, QF)	2-1
Sat May 10	Leeds United (A, SF)	0-1

FA YOUTH CUP

Tue Dec 3	Colchester United (H)	2-0
Wed Jan 15	Millwall (A)	1-2

151

FIRST-TEAM FIXTURES

(FA Women's National Premier League except where indicated)

Thu Aug 8	Fulham (N*, Community Shield)	2-2
	Lost 3-1 on pens	
Sat Aug 31	Tranmere Rovers (H)	6-0
Sun Sep 8	Leeds United (A)	6-3
Wed Sep 11	Birmingham City (H)	5-0
Tue Sep 24	Gomrukcu Baku (H, UEFA Cup)	6-0
Thu Sep 26	Levante UD (H, UEFA Cup)	2-1
Sun Sep 29	Eendracht Alst (H, UEFA Cup)	7-0
Sun Oct 6	Everton (H)	3-2
Sun Oct 13	Sheffield Wednesday (H, League Cup R1)	11-0
Sun Oct 20	Brighton & Hove Albion (H)	4-1
Wed Oct 23	Birmingham City (A)	0-1
Sat Nov 2	CSK Samara (A, UEFA Cup QF)	2-0
Thu Nov 7	Fulham (H)	1-2
Sun Nov 10	Leeds United (A, League Cup R2)	3-0
Thu Nov 28	CSK Samara (H, UEFA Cup QF)	1-1
Sun Dec 1	Tranmere Rovers (H, League Cup QF)	1-0
Sun Dec 8	Doncaster Belles (H)	3-1
Sun Jan 5	Tranmere Rovers (H, FA Cup R4)	2-0
Sun Jan 26	Wolves (A, FA Cup R5)	4-0
Tue Jan 28	Crystal Palace (H, London County Cup QF)	7-0
Sun Feb 2	Doncaster Belles (A, League Cup SF)	2-1
Sat Feb 8	Aston Villa (H, FA Cup QF)	6-0
Sat Feb 16	Everton (A)	1-0
Sun Mar 2	Southampton (H)	1-0
Sat Mar 8	Nigeria (A, Charity Match)	1-5
Sun Mar 23	Charlton Athletic (A, FA Cup SF)	0-1
Sun Mar 30	Fulham (N+, League Cup Final)	1-1 $
Sat Apr 5	Hjorring (A, UEFA Cup SF)	1-3
Sat Apr 12	Leeds United (H)	4-1
Tues Apr 15	Fulham (A)	1-4
Sun Apr 20	Tranmere Rovers (A)	7-1
Wed Apr 23	Brighton & Hove Albion (A)	5-1
Sun Apr 27	Hjorring (H, UEFA Cup SF)	1-5
Wed Apr 30	Southampton (A)	3-1
Sun May 4	Doncaster Belles (A)	1-1
Thu May 8	Charlton Athletic (H)	1-2
Sun May 11	Charlton Athletic (A)	1-0

* played at Brisbane Road

+ played at Swindon

$ lost on penalties

FA Womens National Premier League

	P	W	D	L	F	A	Pts
Fulham	18	16	2	0	63	13	49*
Doncaster Belles	18	13	2	3	34	19	41
ARSENAL	18	13	1	4	53	21	40
Charlton Athletic	18	10	4	4	44	20	34
Birmingham City	18	6	3	9	26	31	21
Tranmere Rovers	18	6	3	9	25	48	21
Leeds United	18	5	4	9	33	42	19
Everton	18	5	1	12	18	38	16
Southampton	18	2	5	11	10	30	11
Brighton & Hove Albion	18	1	1	16	18	62	4

*Fulham deducted one point for fielding an ineligible player

APPEARANCES (SUBS IN BRACKETS) AND GOALS

	Premiership	UEFA Champions League	League Cup	FA Cup	Total
JAYNE LUDLOW	18 (0) 15	6 (0) 4	5 (0) 6	4 (0) 6	33 (0) 31
ANGIE BANKS	18 (0) 14	5 (0) 4	5 (0) 3	4 (0) 2	32 (0) 23
EMMA BYRNE	18 (0) –	6 (0) –	5 (0) –	4 (0) –	33 (0) –
LEANNE CHAMP	18 (0) –	4 (1) –	4 (0) –	4 (0) –	28 (1) –
CLARE WHEATLEY	18 (0) –	6 (0) 2	5 (0) –	4 (0) –	33 (0) 2
CIARA GRANT	16 (0) 7	6 (0) 2	5 (0) 2	3 (0) 1	30 (0) 12
ELLEN MAGGS	16 (1) 5	6 (0) 3	3 (0) 3	2 (0) –	27 (0) 11
KIRSTY PEALLING	15 (0) 2	5 (0) –	4 (0) –	4 (0) –	28 (0) 2
SIAN WILLIAMS	14 (3) –	5 (0) –	3 (2) –	1 (2) –	23 (7) –
JULIE FLETCHER	14 (3) –	6 (0) –	3 (0) –	4 (0) –	27 (3) –
YVONNE TRACY	12 (1) –	3 (2) –	5 (0) –	4 (0) –	24 (3) –
PAULINE MacDONALD	10 (0) 2	3 (1) 1	3 (0) –	4 (0) –	20 (1) 3
FAYE WHITE	4 (1) 1	3 (0) 1	– – –	– – –	7 (1) 2
AYSHEA MARTYN	2 (8) 1	– (2) –	1 (3) 1	2 (2) 1	5 (15) 3
LIANNE SANDERSON	2 (3) 4	– (1) –	– – –	– – –	2 (4) 4
ALEX SCOTT	1 (10) –	– (3) 1	1 (3) –	– (3) 1	2 (19) 2
MICHELLE O'BRIEN	1 (5) 1	– (1) –	– – –	– – –	1 (6) 1
GEMMA RITCHIE	– (1) –	– (1) –	1 (0) 1	– – –	1 (2) 1
ANITA ASANTE	1 (4) –	2 (0) –	1 (1) –	– (1) –	4 (6) –
HAYLEY KEMP	– – –	– – –	– – –	– – –	– (1) –
LISA BURROWS	– – –	– – –	– (1) –	– (1) –	– (2) –
SHEUNEEN TA	– – –	– – –	– (1)–	– – –	– (1) –
Own goals	– (0) 1	– – –	– 2	– (0) 1	– (0) 4

OFFICIALS

VIC AKERS General Manager
DANNY O'SHEA Assistant Manager
CLARE WHEATLEY Development Manager
CIARA GRANT Assistant Development Officer
ANGIE BANKS Assistant Development Officer
JAYNE LUDLOW Medical Oficer

Aston Villa

Villa Park, Trinity Road,
Birmingham, B6 6HE
Tel 0121 327 2299
Ticket Information 0121 327 5353
Website www.avfc.co.uk

Aston Villa's season in brief...
• Villa's Intertoto Cup campaign comes to an end with a 2-0 defeat against Lille in the semi-finals.
• Three defeats in the first four games see Villa drop to 16th place at the start of September.
• A run of good form in November culminates with a 4-1 victory over West Ham United that lifts the Villans to 11th place in the Premiership.
• Icelandic midfielder Joey Gudjonsson signs on loan from Real Betis on 20 January.
• Villa confirm their Premiership surivial with a 1-0 victory over Sunderland in their penultimate game of the season.

In 2002-03 Premiership

P	W	D	L	F:A	Pts	Pos
38	12	9	17	42:47	45	16th

Against Arsenal

Arsenal 3	Aston Villa 1
Pires, Henry (2)	Hitzlsperger

Aston Villa 1	Arsenal 1
Toure (og)	Ljungberg

Top goalscorer Dion Dublin 9

FA Cup
Lost to Blackburn Rovers, 1-4
4th round (H)

Worthington Cup
Lost to Liverpool, 6th round (H) 3-4

Birmingham City

St Andrews, Birmingham, B9 4NH
Tel 0121 772 0101
Website www.bcfc.com

Birmingham City's season in brief...
• Blues prepare for their top-flight return with a busy summer on the transfer market. Aliou Cisse, Robbie Savage and Kenny Cunningham are among the new arrivals at St Andrews.
• Steve Bruce's team kick-off the season with two defeats but a win against Villa in mid-December lifts the Premiership newcomers to 9th place.
• French World Cup winner Christophe Dugarry is among a host of transfer-window signings who join Birmingham in January.
• Blues beat Liverpool 2-1 in February, ending a run that had seen them take just one point from eight Premiership games.
• Steve Bruce's team rally to collect 12 points from a possible 15 in April and thereby stave off the threat of relegation.

In 2002-03 Premiership

P	W	D	L	F:A	Pts	Pos
38	13	9	16	41:49	48	13th

Against Arsenal

Arsenal 2	Birmingham City 0
Henry, Wiltord	

Birmingham City 0	Arsenal 4
	Henry (2),
	Pires, Lauren

Top goalscorer Clinton Morrison 6

FA Cup
Lost to Fulham, 3rd round (A) 1-3

Worthington Cup
Lost to Preston North End, 0-2
3rd round (H)

Blackburn Rovers

Ewood Park, Blackburn, BB2 4JF
Tel 01254 698 888
Ticket line 01254 671 666
Website www.rovers.co.uk

Blackburn Rovers' season in brief...
• Summer signing Dwight Yorke earns Rovers their first win of the season with the only goal of the game against Birmingham at St Andrews in August.
• Rovers lose out to Celtic in an entertaining UEFA Cup clash, having disposed of CSKA Sofia in the previous round.
• Graeme Souness's men progress to the semi-final of the Worthington Cup with a 2-0 win against Wigan. However, their defence of the cup comes to an end at the hands of Manchester United over two legs.
• A 4-0 win against Spurs on the final day of the season ensures that Rovers clinch a place in the UEFA Cup for 2003/04.

In 2002-03 Premiership

P	W	D	L	F:A	Pts	Pos
38	16	12	10	52:43	60	6th

Against Arsenal

Arsenal 1	Blackburn Rovers 2
Edu	Edu (og), Yorke

Blackburn Rovers 2	Arsenal 0
Duff, Tugay	

Top goalscorer Damien Duff 9

FA Cup

Lost to Sunderland,   2-2
4th round (A)   (*0-3 on pens)

Worthington Cup

Lost to Manchester   2-4 (agg)
United, semi-final

Bolton Wanderers

Reebok Stadium, Burnden Way,
Lostock, Bolton, BL6 6JW
Tel 01204 673 673
Ticket office 01204 673601
Website www.bwfc.co.uk

Bolton Wanderers' season in brief...

• Wanderers' first away victory of the
season comes against Manchester
United, but despite their win at Old
Trafford, the Trotters sit bottom of the
table at the end of October.
• A late Michael Ricketts goal at Upton
Park on 21 December earns Sam
Allardyce's men a vital point in the bat-
tle to avoid relegation.
• Bolton record their best Premiership
result of the season with a 5-2 victory
over Birmingham City at the Reebok
in February.
• Jay-Jay Okocha scores March's
Premiership goal of the Month in a
crucial 1-0 victory over resurgent
West Ham United.
• A 2-1 win over Middlesbrough sees
Bolton avoid relegation on the final
day of the season.

In 2002-03 Premiership

P	W	D	L	F:A	Pts	Pos
38	10	14	14	41:51	44	17th

Against Arsenal

Arsenal 2	Bolton Wanderers 1
Henry, Kanu	Farrelly

Bolton Wanderers 2	Arsenal 2
Djorkaeff, Keown (og)	Wiltord, Pires

Top goalscorer Jay-Jay Okocha and
Henrik Pedersen 7

FA Cup

Lost to Sunderland,   0-2
3rd round replay (H)

Worthington Cup

Lost to Bury, 2nd round (H)   0-1

Charlton Athletic

The Valley, Floyd Road, Charlton,
London, SE7 8BL
Tel 020 8333 4000
Ticket office 020 8333 4010
Website www.cafc.co.uk

Charlton Athletic's season in brief...

• Alan Curbishley's team end August
with a 2-0 win at West Ham which
takes them fifth in the Premiership.
• Four consecutive wins in October
and November, including a 2-0
victory over Liverpool at The Valley,
sees Charlton climb from 17th place
to 11th.
• Charlton are eliminated from the
FA Cup with a 3-0 defeat against
Fulham in the 3rd round but respond
with a run of four successive
Premiership victories.
• A run of eight defeats in the final ten
games sees the Addicks drop to 12th
in the final standings.

In 2002-03 Premiership

P	W	D	L	F:A	Pts	Pos
38	14	7	17	45:56	49	12th

Against Arsenal

Charlton 0	Arsenal 3
	Henry, Wiltord, Edu

Arsenal 2	Charlton 0
Jeffers, Pires	

Top goalscorer Jason Euell 10

FA Cup

Lost to Fulham, 4th round (A)   0-3

Worthington Cup

Lost to Oxford United, (H)   0-0
2nd round (5-6 on pens)

Chelsea

Stamford Bridge, London, SW16 1HS
Tel 020 7385 5545
Ticket office 09068 121 011
Website www.chelseafc.co.uk

Chelsea's season in brief...

• Blues' UEFA Cup campaign comes
to an end with a 4-2 reverse against
FK Viking.
• Chelsea remain unbeaten in
November, rising up the Premiership
to a high of second place. However,
their good run comes to an end with a
1-0 defeat in a Worthington Cup quarter-final against Manchester United.
• Claudio Ranieri's men score five
goals against Manchester City without
reply to record their biggest win of the
season in March.
• Blues beat Liverpool 2-1 at
Stamford Bridge on the final day
of the season to earn a place in the
Champions League.

In 2002-03 Premiership

P	W	D	L	F:A	Pts	Pos
38	19	10	9	68:38	67	4th

155

Against Arsenal

Chelsea 1	Arsenal 1
Zola	Toure

Arsenal 3	Chelsea 2
Desailly (og),	Stanic, Petit
van Bronckhorst,	
Henry	

Top goalscorer Gianfranco Zola 14

FA Cup

Lost to Arsenal,   1-3
6th round replay (H)

Worthington Cup

Lost to Manchester   0-1
United, 5th round (A)

Everton

Goodison Park, Liverpool, L4 4EL
Tel 0151 330 2200
Ticket Information 09068 121 599
Website www.evertonfc.com

Everton's season in brief...
• Former Gunner Kevin Campbell secures Everton's first win of the season with the only goal of the game against Sunderland at the Stadium of Light in August.
• Wayne Rooney comes off the bench to score a last-minute winner against champions Arsenal on 19 October.
• A crowd of 40,000 attends Goodison to watch the Toffees beat West Brom 1-0 to record a sixth successive Premiership victory that takes them up to third in the table on 23 November.
• Shrewsbury Town's Nigel Jemson scores a late goal to eliminate Everton from the FA Cup in the 3rd round.
• A Ruud van Nistelrooy penalty sees

Everton lose their final game 2-1 to Manchester United and thus miss out on sixth place and a UEFA Cup spot.

In 2002-03 Premiership

P	W	D	L	F:A	Pts	Pos
38	17	8	13	48:49	59	7th

Against Arsenal

Everton 2	Arsenal 1
Radzinski, Rooney	Ljungberg

Arsenal 2	Everton 1
Cygan, Vieira	Rooney

Top goalscorer Tomasz Radzinski 10

FA Cup

Lost to Shrewsbury   1-2
Town, 3rd round (A)

Worthington Cup

Lost to Chelsea, 4th round (A)   1-4

Fulham

Craven Cottage, Stevenage Road, Fulham, London, SW6 6HH
(Fulham are currently ground sharing with Queen's Park Rangers at Loftus Road)
Tel 020 7893 8383
Website www.fulhamfc.co.uk

Fulham's season in brief...
• Former Arsenal midfielder Junichi Inamoto scores a hat-trick in the second leg of the Intertoto Cup final as Fulham beat Bologna 3-1 to clinch a place in the UEFA Cup.
• The Cottagers kick off their Premiership campaign with a 4-1 win over Bolton at Loftus Road.
• Wigan end Fulham's interest in the Worthington Cup on 4 December. Defeat against Wigan came just a

week after Hertha Berlin had knocked Jean Tigana's side out of Europe.
• Tigana parts company with Fulham in April. Chris Coleman takes charge for the final five games of the season.
• Fulham take ten points from a possible 15 to avert the threat of relegation and Coleman is given the manager's job on a permanent basis.

In 2002-03 Premiership

P	W	D	L	F:A	Pts	Pos
38	13	9	16	41:50	48	14th

Against Arsenal

Fulham 0	Arsenal 1
	Marlet (og)

Arsenal 2	Fulham 1
Pires (2)	Malbranque

Top goalscorer Steed Malbranque 6

FA Cup

Lost to Burnley,   0-3
5th round replay (A)

Worthington Cup

Lost to Wigan Athletic,   1-2
4th round (A)

Leeds United

Elland Road, Leeds, LS11 0ES
Tel 0113 226 6000
Ticket office 09068 121 680
Website www.lufc.co.uk

Leeds United's season in brief...
• Terry Venables' team start the season with an impressive 3-0 victory over Manchester City at Elland Road.
• Jonathan Woodgate and Lee Bowyer depart for Newcastle and West Ham

respectively during the January transfer window.

• Terry Venables leaves the club and is replaced by Peter Reid who initially takes charge until the end of the season. He is later given the job permanently.

• Sheffield United end Leeds' hopes of FA Cup glory with a 1-0 win at Bramall Lane in the quarter-final.

• Mark Viduka's goal earns Leeds victory at Highbury on 3 May and clinches the Yorkshire side's place in the Premiership for 2003/04.

In 2002-03 Premiership

P	W	D	L	F:A	Pts	Pos
38	14	5	19	58:57	47	15th

Against Arsenal

Leeds 1	Arsenal 4
Kewell	Kanu (2), Toure, Henry

Arsenal 2	Leeds United 3
Henry, Bergkamp	Kewell, Harte, Viduka

Top goalscorer Mark Viduka 20

FA Cup

Lost to Sheffield United, 0-1
6th round (A)

Worthington Cup

Lost to Sheffield United, 1-2
3rd round (A)

Liverpool

Anfield Road, Liverpool, L4 0TH
Tel 0151 263 2361
Ticket and Match Information
0151 260 9999
Website www.liverpoolfc.tv

Liverpool's season in brief...

• Gerard Houllier's team start the season in fine form and remain unbeaten in the Premiership until 9 November when Middlesbrough beat them 1-0 at The Riverside.

• Liverpool's Champions League campaign comes to an end with a 3-3 draw against Swiss side Basle.

• Goals from Steve Gerrard and Michael Owen earn the Merseysiders a 2-0 win in the Worthington Cup Final against Manchester United.

• Celtic end Liverpool's interest in the UEFA Cup with a 3-1 aggregate win in the quarter-finals.

• Defeat in the final match of the season against Chelsea at Stamford Bridge sees the Reds miss out on a lucrative Champions League place.

In 2002-03 Premiership

P	W	D	L	F:A	Pts	Pos
38	18	10	10	61:41	64	5th

Against Arsenal

Arsenal 1	Liverpool 1
Henry	Murphy

Liverpool 2	Henry 2
Riise, Heskey	Pires, Bergkamp

Top goalscorer Michael Owen 24

FA Cup

Lost to Crystal Palace, 0-2
4th round replay (H)

Worthington Cup

Won competition, beating Manchester United 2-0 in the final.

Manchester City

City of Manchester Stadium, Rowsley Street, Manchester
Tel 0161 232 3000
Ticket office 0161 226 2224
Website www.mcfc.co.uk

Manchester City's season in brief...

• City record their third successive victory with a 3-1 triumph over neighbours United in the last ever derby game at Maine Road in November.

• Kevin Keegan's team bow out of both domestic Cup competitions at the first hurdle as first Wigan in the Worthington Cup and then Liverpool in the FA Cup beat the Blues.

• City's final game at Maine Road ends in a 1-0 defeat against Cup finalists Southampton.

• The Blues are officially the Premiership's best-behaved team, earning them a place in the UEFA Cup through the Fair Play draw.

In 2002-03 Premiership

P	W	D	L	F:A	Pts	Pos
38	15	6	17	47:54	51	9th

Against Arsenal

Arsenal 2	Manchester City 1
Wiltord, Henry	Anelka

Manchester City 1	Arsenal 5
Anelka	Bergkamp, Pires, Henry, Campbell, Vieira

Top goalscorer Nicolas Anelka 13

FA Cup

Lost to Liverpool, 3rd round (H) 0-1

Worthington Cup

Lost to Wigan Athletic,　　　0-1
3rd round (A)

Manchester United

Sir Matt Busby Way, Old Trafford,
Manchester, M16 0RA
Tel 0161 868 8000
Ticket and Match Information
0161 868 8020
Website www.manutd.com

Manchester United's season in brief...
• Consecutive defeats to Bolton
(home) and Leeds (away) see United
drop to ninth in the Premiership in
mid-September.
• A run of eight back-to-back victories
in all competitions during November
and December, sees the Reds revive
their title challenge and qualify for the
semi-finals of the Worthington Cup.
• United lose out to Liverpool 2-0 in
the Worthington Cup Final at the
Millennium Stadium.
• Holders Real Madrid knock Alex
Ferguson's team out of the
Champions League with a 6-5 aggregate victory in the quarter-finals.
• United win the Premiership crown
with a run of nine victories in their final
ten games of the season.

In 2002-03 Premiership

P	W	D	L	F:A	Pts	Pos
38	25	8	5	74:34	83	1st

Against Arsenal

Manchester United 2	Arsenal 0
Veron, Scholes	

Arsenal 2	Manchester United 2
Henry (2)	van Nistelrooy, Giggs

Top goalscorer Ruud van Nistelrooy 25

FA Cup

Lost to Arsenal, 5rd round (H)　　0-2

Worthington Cup

Lost to Liverpool, Final (N)　　0-2

Middlesbrough

BT Cellnet Riverside Stadium,
Middlesbrough, TS3 6RS
Tel 01642 877 700
Ticket Information 01642 877 809
Website www.mfc.co.uk

Middlesbrough's season in brief...
• New signing Massimo Maccarone
scores twice on his home debut as
Boro clinch their second point of the
season with a 2-2 draw against Fulham.
• Boro move up third on 5 October
when they record a third successive
victory in the Premiership, beating
Bolton 2-0 at The Riverside.
• Juninho's goal in the 1-1 draw
against Everton in March is the
Brazilian's first since his return to
Teesside the previous summer.
• Boro complete their home fixtures in
the Premiership with a 5-1 victory over
Tottenham Hotspur.

In 2002-03 Premiership

P	W	D	L	F:A	Pts	Pos
38	13	10	15	48:44	49	11th

Against Arsenal

Arsenal 2	Middlesbrough 0
Campbell, Pires	

Middlesbrough 0	Arsenal 2
	Wiltord, Henry

Top goalscorer Massimo Maccarone 9

FA Cup

Lost to Chelsea, 3rd round (A)　　0-1

Worthington Cup

Lost to Ipswich Town,　　　1-3
3rd round (A)

Newcastle United

St James' Park, Newcastle-upon-Tyne,
NE1 4ST
Tel 0191 201 8400
Box office 0191 261 1571
Website www.nufc.co.uk

Newcastle United's season in brief...
• The Magpies lose three of their first
five Premiership games and sit 19th in
the table in mid-September.
• Bobby Robson's team lose their first
three Champions League games but
take maximum points from their
remaining fixtures and thereby earn
qualification for the next phase.
• A mid-season revival sees Newcastle
move into contention for the title after
a run that sees them drop just two
points from a possible 27.
• A 2-0 defeat against Barcelona at St
James' ends Newcastle's Champions
League campaign.
• A goal from Portuguese midfielder
Hugo Viana earns Newcastle a 1-0
victory over Birmingham City and
secures the club a place in the
2003/04 Champions League.

In 2002-03 Premiership

P	W	D	L	F:A	Pts	Pos
38	21	6	11	63:48	69	3rd

Against Arsenal

Arsenal 1	Newcastle United 0
Wiltord	

Newcastle United 1 | Arsenal 1
Robert | Henry

Top goalscorer Alan Shearer 17

FA Cup
Lost to Wolverhampton 2-3
Wanderers, 3rd round (A)

Worthington Cup
Lost to Everton, 3rd round (A) 3-3
(3-2 on pens)

Southampton

The Friends Provident St Mary's
Stadium, Britannia Road,
Southampton, SO14 5FP
Tel 0870 2200 000
Ticket information 023 8022 8575
Website www.saintsfc.co.uk

Southampton's season in brief...
• Saints win all four of their matches
during October, with James Beattie
netting a hat-trick in the 4-2 win
against Fulham that lifts Gordon
Strachan's team to 10th in the
Premiership.
• Southampton move up to sixth place
with a 1-0 victory over Tottenham on
New Year's Day. The same opponents
are defeated 4-0 three days later in
the 3rd round of the FA Cup.
• Victory over Watford in an FA Cup
semi-final at Villa Park earns Saints
their first Cup final appearance for
27 years.
• Michael Svensson scores the winner
in Saints final Premiership game of the
season against Manchester City.
It is also the final goal scored at
Maine Road.
• Southampton lose out to Arsenal in
the FA Cup Final, with Robert Pires

scoring the only goal of the game.

In 2002-03 Premiership

P	W	D	L	F:A	Pts	Pos
38	13	13	12	43:46	52	8th

Against Arsenal

Southampton 3 | Arsenal 2
Beattie (2), Delgado | Bergkamp,
| Pires

Arsenal 6 | Southampton 1
Pennant (3), | Beattie
Pires (3) |

Top goalscorer James Beattie 23

FA Cup
Lost to Arsenal, Final (N) 0-1

Worthington Cup
Lost to Liverpool, 3rd round (A) 1-3

Sunderland

Sunderland Stadium of Light,
Sunderland, Tyne and Wear, SR5 1SU
Tel 0191 551 5000
Ticket office 0191 551 5151
Website www.safc.com

Sunderland's season in brief...
• Peter Reid's men fail to score in five
of their first seven Premiership games
in 2002/03.
• The Wearsiders put seven goals
past Cambridge City in the 2nd round
of the Worthington Cup and defeat
Arsenal in the next round. However,
they are eliminated by Sheffield United
in round 4.
• Peter Reid is dismissed as manager
in October after seven years in
charge. Howard Wilkinson takes over.
• Wilkinson leaves the club in March

and is replaced by Mick McCarthy.
• McCarthy is unable to avert the
threat of relegation and the Black
Cats have their fate confirmed with a
2-0 defeat against Birmingham City on
12 April.

In 2002-03 Premiership

P	W	D	L	F:A	Pts	Pos
38	4	7	27	21:65	19	20th

Against Arsenal

Arsenal 3 | Sunderland 1
Kanu (2), Vieira | Craddock

Sunderland 0 | Arsenal 4
| Henry, Ljungberg (3)

Top goalscorer Kevin Phillips 6

FA Cup
Lost to Watford, 5th round (H) 0-1

Worthington Cup
Lost to Sheffield United, 0-2
4th round (A)

Tottenham Hotspur

White Hart Lane, Bill Nicholson Way,
748 High Road, Tottenham, London,
N17 0AP
Tel 020 8365 5000
Ticket information line 09068 100 505
Website www.spurs.co.uk

Tottenham Hotspur season in brief...
• Spurs take ten points from their first
four games and are top of the
Premiership at the start of September.
• Southampton eliminate Spurs
from the FA Cup with a 4-0 win at
St Mary's.
• Robbie Keane's second-half hat-trick
against Everton at White Hart Lane on

159

12 January clinches a 4-3 victory and boosts Spurs' challenge for a UEFA Cup spot.
• Glenn Hoddle's team drop to tenth after losing their final three games, conceding 11 goals in the process.

In 2002-03 Premiership

P	W	D	L	F:A	Pts	Pos
38	14	8	16	51:62	50	10th

Against Arsenal

Arsenal 3	Tottenham Hotspur 0
Henry,	
Ljungberg,	
Wiltord	

Tottenham Hotspur 1	Arsenal 1
Ziege	Pires

Top goalscorer Teddy Sheringham 13

FA Cup
Lost to Southampton,   0-4
3rd round (A)

Worthington Cup
Lost to Burnley, 3rd round (A)   1-2

West Bromwich Albion

The Hawthorns, West Bromwich,
B71 4LF
Tel 0121 525 8888
Website www.wba.premiumtv.co.uk

West Bromwich Albion's season in brief...
• The Baggies start the season with three consecutive defeats but their fortunes revive and a trio of wins takes them up to 7th in the Premiership by mid-September.
• A 3-1 reverse against Manchester United at Old Trafford sends Gary

Megson's team to the foot of the table on 11 January.
• Watford end West Brom's interest in the FA Cup with a 1-0 win at Vicarage Road.
• A run of nine defeats in 10 games between 19 February and 26 April sees the Baggies relegated.

In 2002-03 Premiership

P	W	D	L	F:A	Pts	Pos
38	6	8	24	29:65	26	19th

Against Arsenal

Arsenal 5	WBA 2
Cole, Lauren,	Dobie, Roberts
Wiltord (2),	
Aliadiere	

WBA 1	Arsenal 2
Dichio	Jeffers, Henry

Top goalscorer Scott Dobie and Daniele Dichio 5

FA Cup
Lost to Watford, 4th round (A)   0-1

Worthington Cup
Lost to Wigan Athletic,   1-3
2nd round (A)

West Ham United

Boleyn Ground, Green Street,
Upton Park, London, E13 9AZ
Tel 020 8548 2748
Ticket office 020 8548 2700
Website www.whufc.co.uk

West Ham United's season in brief...
• Hammers fail to win any of their first six Premiership games.
• Seven defeats in ten games leaves Glenn Roeder's team

bottom of the table at Christmas.
• Roeder is one of the Premiership's busiest managers during the January transfer window – signing Les Ferdinand, Lee Bowyer and Rufus Brevett.
• A spring time revival sees Hammers win three times in four games as Roeder is named Barclaycard Manager of the Month for March.
• A draw at Birmingham City on the last day of the season is not enough to save West Ham's Premiership status and they are relegated.

In 2002-03 Premiership

P	W	D	L	F:A	Pts	Pos
38	10	12	16	42:59	42	18th

Against Arsenal

West Ham United 2	Arsenal 2
J Cole, Kanoute	Henry,
	Wiltord

Arsenal 3	West Ham United 1
Henry (3)	Defoe

Top goalscorer Paolo Di Canio 9

FA Cup
Lost to Manchester United,   0-6
4th round (A)

Worthington Cup
Lost to Oldham Athletic,   0-1
3rd round (H)